Mary Colter

Mary Elizabeth Jane Colter

Mary Colter

BUILDER UPON THE RED EARTH

by Virginia L. Grattan

GRAND CANYON NATURAL HISTORY ASSOCIATION
GRAND CANYON, ARIZONA / 1992

1992 EDITION

ISBN 0-938216-45-7

Library of Congress Catalog Card Number 92-072441

Composed and Printed in the United States of America

♻ Printed on Archival Quality Recycled Paper

First published by Northland Press

Flagstaff, Arizona in 1980

Permission to reprint the photographs, drawings, and letters on the following pages has been granted by: Fred Harvey Transportation Company: 40-42, 47; *The Hotel Monthly:* 85, 86, 89; The Museum of New Mexico: 24, 55, 56, 105, 124; The National Park Service: Foreword, 36, 65, 68, 72, 74, 77, 79, 81, 83, 87, 88, 92, 93, 103-104; Mr. and Mrs. Preston P. Patraw: 112; Santa Fe Railway: 7 right, 23, 70, 71, 96; Mary Larkin Smith: frontispiece, 5, 7 left, 116; University of Arizona Special Collections: x, 9, 11, 12, 15, 16, 17, 18, 27, 29, 30, 31, 33, 34, 35, 38, 40, 43, 45, 49, 51, 53, 58, 60, 61, 62, 63, 66, 98, 122.

Contents

List of Illustrations

Foreword

EVERY NOW AND THEN a book comes along whose value exceeds the dollar figures tallied on the bottom line. Such a work is *Mary Colter: Builder Upon the Red Earth*, the biography of a remarkable woman who worked on the frontier—both literally and figuratively—and succeeded at "a man's job" in "a man's world."

After four printings, with some 7,000 copies in circulation, Colter's story went out of print in 1989. During the intervening years we have received numerous inquiries about the book, and suffered through expressions of regret and indignation when we answered that it was no longer available.

A significant body of Mary Colter's work may still be seen and enjoyed at Grand Canyon National Park. It seemed logical, then, that Grand Canyon Natural History Association should bring the book back into print. Only minor changes have been made in this edition for the sake of correction or clarification. The original book remains substantially unchanged.

It is with pleasure that we reintroduce this book to the marketplace.

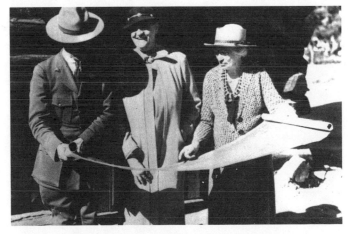

(Left to Right) M.R. Tillotson, Grand Canyon National Park Superintendent, Mrs. Harold Ickes, wife of the Secretary of the Interior, and Mary Colter, circa 1935.

Pam Frazier
Grand Canyon Natural History Association
June 1992

West view of Hermit's Rest

CHAPTER ONE

Beginnings
1869 - 1910

T HE GRAND CANYON is still the showplace for Mary Elizabeth Jane Colter's art. Her stone buildings stand on the south rim looking as old as the canyon itself, resembling ancient structures left by the tribes that inhabited the region long before Columbus. Hermits Rest, the Lookout, and Bright Angel Lodge overlook the canyon where, a mile below, rests Phantom Ranch. In the village is Hopi House and twenty-five miles to the east, the Watchtower. Although many of the buildings Mary Colter designed or decorated in her lifetime are now gone, these at Grand Canyon remain as evidence of her originality.

A schoolteacher in St. Paul, Minnesota, in the 1890s, Mary Colter became an architect, designer, and decorator for the Fred Harvey Company in 1902. As the Santa Fe Railway pushed west, the Fred Har-vey Company opened hotels and restaurants next to the stations to accommodate an increasing number of passengers. It was the Santa Fe Railway that brought the Fred Harvey Company and Mary Colter to Grand Canyon. And with her came a new style of architecture.

When Colter began her career with Fred Harvey, American architecture still followed the fashions of Europe. The Victorian gingerbread style was passing from favor, being replaced by the classic columns of Roman and Renaissance models, foreign styles superimposed on the American landscape. But Colter's architecture grew out of the land, out of the richness of its history. Her buildings pay homage to the early inhabitants of the region. Native Americans had inhabited the land for a millennia and had built upon it with the materials at hand, creating dwellings in harmony with the environment. Hispanic Americans brought with them Spanish culture and tradition and shaped their buildings in the new land by their memories of Old Spain. Colter's buildings had their roots in the history of the land. She designed not replicas of these earlier buildings, but re-creations, buildings that captured the essence of the past. She built ancient-looking Indian "ruins" at Grand Canyon — the Watchtower and the Lookout — after the authentic ruins of Indian towers and dwellings found in the Southwest; Hopi House after the Hopi dwellings at Oraibi, Arizona; and Bright Angel Lodge in the style of early pioneer buildings at Grand Canyon. La Posada at Winslow was a romantic interpretation of the Spanish rancho style of early Mexican settlers in the Southwest.

Colter's buildings have the simplicity, even crudity, of the early architecture after which they were patterned. For her there was charm and dignity in these rustic beginnings. Like other architects in California and the Southwest just before the turn of the century, Mary Colter was more interested in rediscovering the cultural heritage of the region than in imitating European styles. Her buildings fit their setting because they grew out of the history of the land. They belonged.

Although she always considered St. Paul her hometown, Mary Colter was born in Pittsburgh, Pennsylvania. Her Irish parents, William and Rebecca Crozier Colter, had immigrated to St. Paul because William had relatives there; their first daughter, Harriet Brierly Colter, was born there in 1863. Rebecca, however, wanted to live closer to her relatives in Pittsburgh, and after the birth of Harriet, the Colters moved there. They opened the Hats, Caps, and Clothing Store at Butler near Forty-fourth Street with ten thousand dollars that William had made in the furniture business. Rebecca worked as a milliner in the store with her husband until their second child, Mary Elizabeth Jane Colter, was born, on April 4, 1869.

But William was not content in Pittsburgh. The family moved to Texas, and then again to Colorado. Finally, they moved back to St. Paul, settling there permanently in 1880 when Mary was eleven.

The city of St. Paul had grown up around a pioneer's mill built in 1821 on the banks of the Mississippi River in Sioux Indian territory. In 1880 when the Colters settled there, the city had 40,000 residents and boasted of an opera house. There was still a large Indian population in the area, and as a young girl, Mary became interested in Indian art when a friend gave her some Sioux drawings. Later, a smallpox epidemic swept the Indian community. Wanting to prevent the spread of disease, Mary's mother burned all the Indian articles in the house. But the Sioux drawings were so precious to Mary that she hid them and saved them from destruction. She kept them the rest of her life.

The railroads that were so important to Mary Colter's later career were part of her childhood as

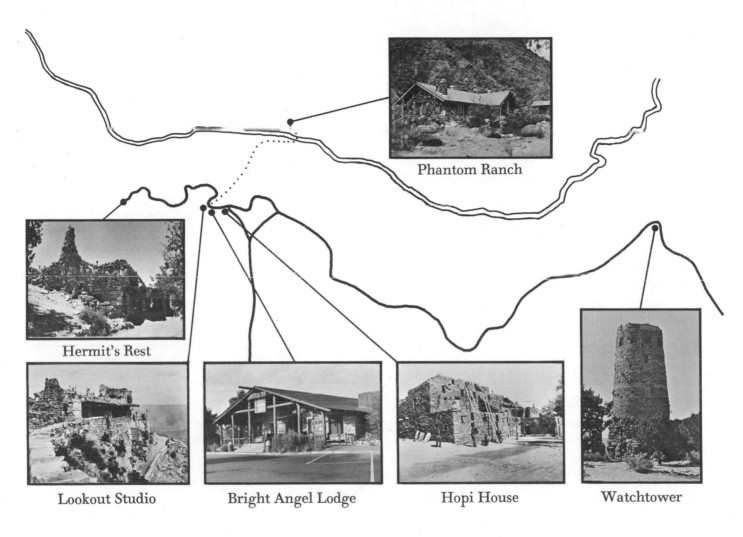

Phantom Ranch

Hermit's Rest

Lookout Studio

Bright Angel Lodge

Hopi House

Watchtower

Colter's major buildings at Grand Canyon

well. President Chester Arthur and General U. S. Grant came for the ceremonies the year the Northern Pacific Railway was completed, linking St. Paul to Portland, Oregon. That was in 1883, the year Mary graduated from high school.

School was important to Mary; there her interest in art grew. The curriculum of the St. Paul public schools required art and music for every student throughout elementary school. Classes included clay modeling, basket weaving, and object drawing. Students drew freehand at the blackboard while their classmates watched. Reading, arithmetic, geography, and "physical culture" were also required in elementary school, but art was considered equally important. St. Paul High School had a more traditional program, offering four languages — Latin, Greek, German, and French — and a number of courses in science and mathematics, as well as history, music, literature, and art.

Encouraged by her high school training, Mary wanted a career in art. It was three more years, however, before she gained her parents' approval to attend art school — not, in fact, until after her father's death. Besides possessing an obvious artistic talent, Mary had a strong and determined personality. Unlike Harriet, her quiet and withdrawn older sister, Mary knew what she wanted and pursued it. She was fourteen when she graduated from high school, and although some art schools would accept students that young, her parents undoubtedly felt that she was too young to go away to school. Then, too, the school she wanted to attend was in San Fran-

cisco, two thousand miles away, a long distance from her family. Another consideration was her father's modest income; at the time of her graduation he was working as a city sewer inspector in St. Paul.

In October of 1886, William Colter died unexpectedly on a trip to St. Peter, Minnesota. He was fifty-three. The cause was listed as "softening of the brain," a sudden thrombosis or blood clot in the brain. His death left a forty-seven-year-old widow and two daughters, aged seventeen and twenty-three, without financial support. Rebecca had worked as a milliner and Harriet was good with needle and thread, but the prospect of supporting three people on the salaries of a milliner and seamstress was not promising. Mary urged them to send her to art school so that she would be able to support them by teaching art. Rebecca reluctantly agreed. With some of the money her father had left, Mary enrolled in art school in San Francisco.

The school she attended was the California School of Design.[1] It was a small school with fewer than seventy students; tuition was $2.50 a month. It offered a four-year program in art and design, and graduates were qualified to teach.

Besides studying art and design at the school, Colter was learning architecture as an apprentice in a local architect's office. In 1887 there were few certified architects in the United States; in 1900 there were only eleven thousand in the whole country. Not until 1901 did California begin licensing architects and establishing standards for the profession. When Colter was a student, few universities even taught

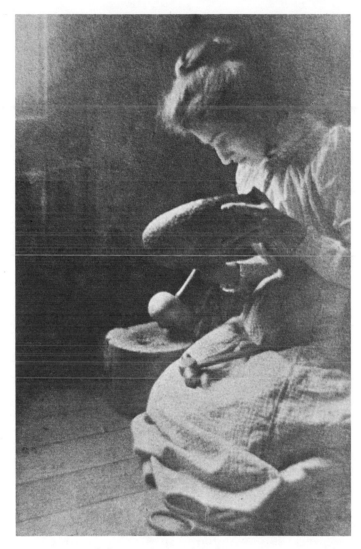

Colter making a bowl, ca. 1892

architecture. The majority of those who wanted to become architects learned their profession as apprentices to practicing architects, as Colter did. It was unusual for a woman to do so, yet designing and decorating buildings was what she dreamed of doing.

During the late 1880s when Colter was an apprentice, local architects were calling for a new building style, one better suited to the California landscape than mere copies of the latest European fashions, like the endless Victorian variations covering the San Francisco hills. They wanted a style "governed altogether by the fitness of design . . . for the purpose for which it is to be erected . . . for the locality where it is to stand . . . for the material chosen, not alone as regards to strength and durability, but with respect to color also."[2] Mary Colter shared these convictions and applied them as guiding principles in her designs. By the time she graduated in 1890, California architects had found a style they considered better suited to the region, one that was patterned after the early California missions. The revival of Spanish architecture in California was beginning.

As a new graduate, Mary's biggest concern was to find a job to help support her mother and sister. Returning to St. Paul to look for a teaching job, she found one in a state-endowed school in nearby Menomonie, Wisconsin, where she taught drawing and architecture for a year. The following year she found a job in St. Paul.

In 1892, at the age of twenty-three, Colter began her fifteen-year teaching career at Mechanic Arts

High School. George Weitbrecht was principal of the small school of 21 teachers and 231 students, all boys. Colter taught freehand and mechanical drawing; after eight years of teaching, her salary rose to ninety dollars a month. With her exuberant energy and ambition, Mary Colter was involved in other activities in addition to teaching high school. She lectured at the University Extension on world history and architecture and participated in the Century Club lectures in Minnesota and Iowa. She also reviewed books in her capacity as literary editor of the St. Paul *Globe*. For her own interest she took courses in archaeology.

On vacation in San Francisco one year, she spent time with a friend who worked in a Fred Harvey gift shop. Mary became acquainted with the manager of the shop and indicated that she would be interested in working for Fred Harvey. Nothing came of that initial contact at the time, but she must have made a favorable impression. In the summer while at her cabin in the Minnesota woods, she was up on the roof making repairs when a Western Union boy from town appeared with a telegram. She was surprised at the length of the message — more than a hundred words. She was even more surprised to read that the Fred Harvey Company was offering her a job.

The Fred Harvey Company had operated the gift shops, newsstands, restaurants, and hotels of the Atchison, Topeka, and Santa Fe Railway since 1876. In the early days of passenger travel, the trains had simply stopped when it was mealtime, leaving passengers to hurry from the train, find something to eat, and hurry back before the train left twenty minutes later. The food at these rail-side eating places had been so unappetizing and exorbitantly priced that Fred Harvey, an enterprising young Englishman, saw an opportunity to provide a needed service. He made an agreement with the Atchison, Topeka, and Santa Fe in which the railway would build and own the station hotels and restaurants while he would manage them and provide good food and service for reasonable prices. The railway's primary interest was transportation; its owners let Fred Harvey manage the hotels and restaurants and reap the profits because they were convinced that these facilities would draw passengers away from competing railways that were without such conveniences.

One of the first Harvey Houses was opened in Holbrook, Arizona, in 1884. It is a good example of Harvey ingenuity and style: next to the station, the restaurant was built into five old boxcars that were painted red and decorated with large geometric Indian designs. The atmosphere inside was of subdued elegance. Tables were set with Irish linen, Sheffield silver, and china from France; fresh cut flowers from California stood beside great pitchers of ice water. The menu featured terrapin, antelope, quail, and blue-point oysters, but the steak dinner was the most popular choice: it cost seventy-five cents. Patrons could select from among five kinds of wine. Refrigerated boxcars made it all possible, bringing the best grade of meat from Kansas City and fresh fruit and vegetables from California.

Mary Colter, ca. 1892   Fred Harvey, ca. 1880

Harvey also insisted on efficient service, making it possible for passengers to eat and be back on the train in thirty minutes. Incoming trains signaled ahead the number of meals required. As the passengers entered the restaurant, an attendant sounded a gong notifying the waitresses to begin serving the meal. A "drink girl" came with the refreshments and knew whether to pour coffee, milk, or tea from the way the waitress had placed the cup: up, down, or on its side.[3] These timesaving efficiencies in service gave the passengers more time to enjoy their meals. The manager urged his guests to take their time, that ample notice would be given before departure of the train. Fred Harvey maintained a restful but "proper" atmosphere in his eating houses; men were expected to wear coats. He set such a standard of taste and decorum that he was often referred to as the "civilizer of the West."[4] As the Santa Fe extended its twelve thousand miles of railway west, the Fred Harvey Company grew with it, opening new Harvey Houses along the way.

Wherever trains stopped in the Southwest, Indians gathered to sell their handwoven blankets and baskets, silver jewelry, and pottery. Passengers from the East were fascinated by these Native Americans. They enjoyed looking at all the wares and bargaining for prices. It wasn't long before the Fred Harvey Company realized that there were economic possibilities in Indian crafts. In 1899, a buyer for the company, Herman Schweizer, commissioned some silver Indian jewelry to be sold in the Fred Harvey shops. Due largely to Schweizer's enthusiasm, the Fred Harvey Company opened an Indian Department in 1901 and launched into the business of merchandising Indian arts. They decided that the new hotel in Albuquerque would have an Indian museum and a salesroom for Indian handicrafts.

When the Fred Harvey Company wired Mary Jane Colter in St. Paul in the summer of 1902 to come to Albuquerque, her first job was to arrange the Indian Building adjoining the new Alvarado Hotel. Fred Harvey "needed a decorator who knew Indian things and had imagination," and that is what they found in Mary Colter. This was to be the beginning of Colter's forty-year association with the Fred Harvey Company and the Santa Fe Railway.

Fred Harvey had died in 1901, but the standards he set were carried on by his sons, Ford and Byron, and his son-in-law, John F. Huckel. These men were convinced that the Southwest had great potential as a tourist area, and they were interested in building a series of fine hotels for vacationers. These were prosperous times for the railway. The president, Edward P. Ripley, described in *The Santa Fe Magazine* as having the "inclinations of a luxurious spendthrift instead of an extreme caretaker," wanted to build the best line of station hotels in the world.[5]

The Harveys hired Charles F. Whittlesey to design the new station hotel in Albuquerque. They wanted a distinctive building, yet one appropriate to the Southwest. For more than ten years, architects in California had been constructing buildings designed like the old missions. It seemed entirely fitting that the station hotel in Albuquerque be in

Bargain hunters in front of the Indian Building, ca. 1912

the mission style, a way station for visitors going to California on the Santa Fe.

The new hotel was named after an early explorer to the Southwest, Hernando de Alvarado. "A great, wide-spreading building like a Spanish mission save for its newness; rough, warm-gray walls and a long procession of arches; all under a red tile roof with many towers — this, facing the distant purple mountains and set against the turquoise sky, is the Alvarado," the Fred Harvey brochure stated. Another advertisement boasted that the new hotel, which opened in 1902, was "the first building in New Mexico to revive the Spanish tradition and thereby make the whole Southwest history-conscious." The hotel had many modern improvements. It was lighted by electricity rather than gas lamps, and it had a thermostat that regulated the steam heat. There were seventy-five rooms, twenty with bath, and the most expensive room was five dollars a day. The hotel contained a club room, barber shop, reading and writing room, and two parlors. A veranda surrounded the exterior of the hotel, which was built around an open courtyard. A two-hundred-foot arcade connected the hotel to the train depot and made the buildings appear to be a long mission.

Along the arcade between the hotel and the depot was the Indian Building. Part of the building was a museum, designed to display a collection of North American Indian arts and crafts, ancient and modern, as well as Eskimo crafts and artifacts from the South Seas. Schweizer and Huckel had spent five years gathering this archaeological collection, which was not for sale. Items were for sale in another section of the building, and it was Mary Colter's job to make them appealing. In the salesrooms, she arranged Indian pots and baskets of every shape and variety on shelves and tables. She piled high stacks of Indian blankets in a myriad of patterns and colors. Indian rugs decorated the floor, and small pottery bowls brightened the mantel of the fireplace. A settee swung on a chain from the ceiling in front of the fireplace, in which a log was always burning.

The Indian Building also contained a replica of a Hopi religious altar respectfully displayed behind locked gates. Henry R. Voth, a Mennonite missionary and anthropologist, had constructed it.[6] Though it was a replica, some Hopis objected to having even a copy made of a religious object. The story was told by the Indians that the Hopi man who had laid the altar was punished and that "in two days he began to swell up. His tongue was swollen and hanging from his mouth."[7] That is, however, the only allegation of misfortune that was ever attributed to the making of the altar.

One of the novel aspects of the Indian Building was the Indian artisans at work. "See patient Navajo squaws weaving blankets, their men engaged in fashioning showy bracelets, rings, and trinkets; Indians from Ácoma and Laguna making pottery; skillful squaws plaiting baskets; see workers in hair, leather, and cloth. Undisturbed by the eager gaze of the tourist, the stoic works on as unconcernedly

A salesroom in the Indian Building, 1905

Navajo women weaving in the Indian workroom

as though in his reservation home," the advertisement read. In one room, the Navajo women sat before their primitive looms weaving brightly colored blankets in strong geometric patterns. They were dressed in full skirts, velvet blouses, and silver necklaces, each with her black hair smoothed back into a knot. The looms were arranged against a painted backdrop of the desert, with small pine boughs overhead and a large Indian rug on the floor. In the corner, a Navajo silversmith worked at a small forge beating out silver jewelry with a hammer.

The Indian Building was so arranged that while the train stopped at the depot, passengers would be drawn to visit the Indian museum and see beautiful displays of native art, then watch the craftsmen and women at work in the Indian workroom, and finally proceed to the curio shop where they could buy a basket, bowl, or blanket to take home as a souvenir. Fred Harvey gathered the best Indian arts and crafts from the Southwest and provided the visitor with a wide selection at reasonable prices. When the Indian Building first opened, there was so little interest in the Native American crafts that Herman Schweizer was often at the station inviting people to visit the museum. But the Indian arts venture of Schweizer and Harvey eventually paid off both for the company and for the Native Americans who had an outlet for their wares.

When the Indian Building opened in 1902, Mary Colter's summer decorating job was over. For the time being, Fred Harvey had no more work to offer her, so she returned to St. Paul and teaching.

The Santa Fe Railway had purchased the bankrupt railroad that ran from Williams, Arizona, to the copper mines at Anita, and the railway was extending the line to the south rim of the Grand Canyon. The only other transportation to Grand Canyon was by stagecoach, a $20 all-day trip from Flagstaff; the railroad made it in less than three hours and charged only $3.95. In 1904 the Fred Harvey Company decided to go ahead with plans for a hotel at Grand Canyon to accommodate the expected influx of tourists. They commissioned Charles F. Whittlesey, the Chicago architect who had designed the Alvarado, to draw up plans for El Tovar, and they contacted Mary Jane Colter to design an Indian building across from it.

The hotel was named for Don Pedro de Tovar, explorer with Coronado in 1540, conqueror of the province of Tusayan, and the first European to learn of the existence of the Grand Canyon. El Tovar was a huge, one-hundred-room, dark wooden structure with a Norwegian or Swiss chalet influence, a hotel to rival the great resort hotels of Europe. Although there were eighty guest rooms, none had a private bath originally. There was, however, a public bath on each of the four floors that could be reserved for a small fee. The hotel had electric lights, with power provided by a steam generator. El Tovar featured a fifteenth-century dining room and several art galleries that sold works by the great landscape painters who came to paint the canyon, Thomas Moran among them. There was a solarium, music room, club room, amusement room, and roof garden. The lobby was decorated with hunting trophies and Indian pottery. To provide the best quality food for its dining rooms, the hotel had its own greenhouse in which to raise vegetables, a herd of cows to provide milk, and chickens for both fresh eggs and poultry. Water was a big problem at the canyon, for it was hauled by train every day from Del Rio, a distance of 120 miles. El Tovar cost $250,000 to build, and it was once referred to as "probably the most expensively constructed and appointed log house in America." It soon became a mecca for travelers from all over the world. Such legendary figures as George Bernard Shaw; Ferdinand Foch, the Marshal of France; and Guglielmo Marconi stayed there. President Taft was entertained at a dinner party there in 1909, and Theodore Roosevelt stayed there while hunting cougar in the canyon.

Hopi House, as Colter's building was called, was built directly across from El Tovar and actually opened a few days before the hotel, on January 1, 1905. Colter wanted to create a building that was appropriate to the setting, something that represented the history of the area and the people who had lived there. Since the Hopis had inhabited the Grand Canyon area for centuries, Colter designed a building in the style of a Hopi dwelling, after those at Oraibi, Arizona. The building was to house the main salesrooms for Fred Harvey Indian arts. Thus, a Hopi building seemed suitable for both the purpose and the location. After Colter's designs were approved, they were sent to the Santa Fe Railway's Western Division offices in Los Angeles, where the working plans were drawn. The building was made of the stone and wood native to the area, and the construction was done largely by Hopi builders. The building featured many terraces with stone steps and ladders made from rough tree limbs connecting one rooftop with another; each rooftop was the porch for the apartment above. Initially, Hopi House was an actual dwelling: some of the Hopis who worked in the building lived on the upper floors.

The interior rooms were in the same primitive style — massive adobe-like walls of rough plaster, with ceilings constructed of log beams with smaller branches lying across them. The floors resembled mud floors but were actually made of cement. Indian baskets and pots were displayed on crude hand-hewn tables. Huge baskets stood on the floors brightened by Navajo rugs. Besides the Indian rooms there was a Spanish-Mexican room with a corner fireplace typical of the Southwest. On the mantel were several carved *bultos* [religious figures] and some wooden candlestick holders. A caballero's saddle, spurs, and sombrero rested on a bench. In a corner nearby stood several old rifles. Other relics included an old leather chest and an ancient wooden plow. There was also a Totem Room that had carved masks and bowls brightly painted by Indians of the Northwest. Colter incorporated two other rare treasures: a sand painting and a Hopi ceremonial altar.

When the Hopi House opened, one room displayed the Harvey museum collection of old Navajo

Hopi House, Grand Canyon, 1905

Hopi House rooftop, 1905

Salesroom in Hopi House (photograph by G. W. Hance)

Blanket weaver and basket maker in the Indian workroom of Hopi House

blankets, a display that had just won the grand prize at the 1904 St. Louis Exposition. The display grew to be the Fred Harvey Fine Arts Collection of nearly five thousand pieces of Indian art collected over the years, primarily by Herman Schweizer — ancient Pueblo pottery, baskets, beadwork, Kachina dolls, jewelry, costumes, and buffalo-hide shields.[8]

Indian artisans could be seen in the workroom of Hopi House making jewelry, pottery, blankets, and other items for sale. In the evening, the Hopis sang traditional songs, and their dancing on the patio at five eventually became a daily event. Hopi House was said to "symbolize the partnership between commercialism and romanticism that typified so much of Fred Harvey architecture." For Mary Colter, it was an opportunity to re-create the distinctive dwelling of an ancient culture and to acquaint the public with the richness and beauty of Native American art.

When Hopi House was completed, Colter once again returned to St. Paul to teach. She still had to support her mother and sister, and she needed to be sure of a steady income. Teaching gave her that security, at least. But she was looking for something more exciting. In 1908 when the Frederick and Nelson Department Store in Seattle, Washington, offered her a job, she took it. She was hired to develop a decoration department and improve the displays.

Harriet and Rebecca Colter moved to Seattle with Mary. They were there only a year when Rebecca became critically ill with pernicious anemia. She died on December 17, 1909. Mary and Harriet brought their mother's body back to St. Paul to be buried in Oakland Cemetery next to their father.

CHAPTER TWO

A New Career
1910 - 1922

THE NEW YEAR, 1910, brought good fortune. Now forty-one years old, Mary Colter was offered a permanent job with the Fred Harvey Company. Her job would be to design and decorate the new Fred Harvey hotels, restaurants, and union station facilities under the supervision of John F. Huckel, vice-president and general manager. The company was expanding its facilities in the Southwest and wanted to be sure that these new buildings maintained the Fred Harvey standard of quality and good taste. It was decided that the company needed a designer among its employees, someone with a background in architecture who knew the Spanish-Indian culture of the Southwest, someone with style and imagination and the strength of personality to see ideas through to actual construction. The man-agers of the company had seen Colter's work in the Indian Building at Albuquerque and Hopi House at Grand Canyon. They knew she had the innate sense of style and taste they were looking for. Having worked with her, they knew she could hold her own with the railroad engineers and contractors and would see that her plans were carried out.

It was certainly unusual for a woman to have such power and influence in a large company; obviously, she had talent and ability. Photographer Laura Gilpin knew her and respected her work. "She was excellent. She was just tops. For instance, with El Navajo at Gallup; the whole decoration of that place was beautiful and very authentic." Others knew her as "a very brilliant lady," "a fine deco-rator." James Marshall described her as "a foremost American architect and interior decorator." Although a railroad man who was used to brightly lit waiting rooms once criticized her as having created "the most poorly illuminated buildings ever built," it was through the use of soft lighting that she produced a restful atmosphere. She re-created a bygone era, a more tranquil age when time moved more slowly. She created pleasant sanctuaries that were removed from the noise and rush of the twentieth century, places where people could rest and regain their composure.

Yet, she might have remained just a talented interior decorator if there hadn't been something remarkable about her personality. Those who knew her differ in their recollections of her. Her critics remember her as a small woman with piercing violet eyes and hair that was never combed. They remember her as a chain-smoker who was outspoken and sometimes even cruel. To her friends, Mary Colter was tall and stately, a wonderful woman, fun to talk to, a happy spirit interested in everything that was going on. Stewart Harvey, grandson of Fred Harvey, remembers her:

She was a determined, positive person. No one was going to push her around. But she was diplomatic. She made it a point to get along well with the Santa Fe Railway architects because they drew the working plans from her building designs. At the same time, they would have to consult her in matters of color and taste. She knew how to bargain. She would get the com-

pany to buy something expensive by agreeing to save on some other item. She had influence with the Harveys, and they would influence the railroad people. This influence she had created herself. She was discreet and knew how to get her way. She had strength. She was an honest, fine person.[1]

She had influence with Frederick Harvey because he was particularly concerned that the buildings represent the Fred Harvey reputation for quality and he "listened to taste and charm." These were Colter's strong suits. "The charm of the hotels was what she did. She knew how to make something look better than it was."[2]

Colter went to work at the Kansas City headquarters of Fred Harvey. She created designs for new buildings and built models of the layout. After additions and alterations were made to suit the company administrators and the preliminary designs were approved, she would draw the floor plans and a rough elevation of the structure and send them to the Santa Fe Railway's engineering department. There the final building plans were drawn by the railroad architects. When the plans were completed and approved by Fred Harvey, the railroad would take bids on the project and hire a contractor to do the construction. The plans for the buildings, as well as the buildings themselves, were owned by the railway, so the plans were signed by the chief engineer of the office, who was licensed by the state. Since Colter had finished her architectural training in

California before that state began licensing architects in 1901, it is unlikely that she ever obtained a license. In her situation it wasn't necessary: the railroad had licensed architects, and they always did the final working plans.

It was obvious to architects of the Santa Fe that "she had spent some time in an architect's office and was well versed in building construction, but not the details or mechanics of planning or engineering."[3] Her competence was in building design, developing a total concept for interior and exterior, and it was this vision that she sketched and created. Later sketches and floor plans of buildings for Indian Gardens and of the Watchtower at Grand Canyon are evidence of her architectural skills. As her work load increased, she had architects working for her in her office.

Colter's title was Architect and Designer, and she was employed by Fred Harvey, but part of her salary was paid by the Santa Fe Railway. The arrangement between Fred Harvey and the Santa Fe was unusual, but it had worked since 1876. Fred Harvey operated the restaurants and hotels of the railway, but owned only the furnishings: beds, curtains, rugs, dishes, and the like. The buildings and the land were both owned by the railway. The arrangement presented difficulties for Colter, at least in the beginning, because she was expected to serve two masters. The Harvey Company would approve a design that would then be altered by the railway engineers, and she would have to marshal her powers of persuasion, influence, or intimidation to have

what she wanted. She had always had a forceful personality, and at Fred Harvey she used it to get the job done.

In 1910, Colter went to New Mexico to design the interiors of the new station hotel at Lamy. Lamy was the transfer point, fifteen miles south of Santa Fe, where passengers going to the city left the main line. Years before, when the railway was being constructed, residents of Santa Fe had favored a rival railroad, so the Santa Fe Railway had bypassed its namesake, leaving it off on a spur. There were enough people passing through Lamy to make it worthwhile for Fred Harvey to have a small hotel built there.

The new hotel, El Ortiz, was designed in the Spanish-Pueblo style by Louis Curtiss, a Kansas City architect. This style, patterned after the early New Mexican adobe buildings, had become the dominant regional style after the University of New Mexico began constructing its buildings in Spanish-Pueblo style in 1905. Also, historic buildings like the Palace of the Governors in Santa Fe were being restored to their original Spanish-Pueblo style. There was a growing interest among residents in restoring the early buildings and in creating new buildings in the old style.

Like the original Spanish-Pueblo buildings, El Ortiz was a one-story structure built around an enclosed courtyard. It was a small inn, having fewer than ten rooms. The lounge had the traditional log-beam viga ceiling and a fireplace on which Colter created a geometric Indian design in the brickwork.

El Ortiz at Lamy, New Mexico, built in 1916

Lobby of El Ortiz with Mexican and Indian furnishings

She furnished the lounge with a heavy carved Mexican table surrounded by brass-studded, straight-backed chairs. The table held a large fern in an Indian pot, and the tile floor was covered with Navajo rugs. On one wall hung a large Mexican *retablo*, a painting of religious figures; against another stood a large carved Spanish chest.

After staying at El Ortiz, Owen Wister, author of *The Virginian*, wrote his compliments to Jacob Stein, the manager. He described El Ortiz as "like a private house of someone who had lavished thought and care upon every nook." Colter must have been pleased, for that was the effect she worked to create. He went on, "In the patio of this hacienda, pigeons were picking in the grass by the little center fountain. This little oasis among the desert hills is a wonder of taste to be looked back upon by the traveler who has stopped there, and forward to by the traveler who is going to stop there. The temptation was to give up all plans and stay a week for the pleasure of living and resting in such a place."

After six years with the Harvey Company, Colter invested her savings in a small house in Altadena, California, where her sister Harriet would live the rest of her life. Harriet settled in Altadena because the mild climate of this hill town near Los Angeles was far kinder to her delicate health than the severe winters of St. Paul. Although Mary maintained an apartment in Kansas City, she traveled a great deal up and down the Santa Fe line working on new building projects. She was frequently in California to buy furnishings for hotels she was decorating and to spend time with Harriet.

⌣•⌣

Tourism had burgeoned at Grand Canyon with the arrival of the railroad, and the Harvey Company soon found it necessary to expand its facilities to accommodate the new influx. The company ran sight-seeing tours along the rim of the canyon in horse-drawn touring stages and had just built Hermit Rim Road along the canyon's edge, west of Bright Angel Camp, at a cost of $185,000. The new road provided eight miles of breathtaking views of the canyon. A terminal was needed at the end of the eight-mile ride, a place where passengers could rest and have refreshments before their return journey. When Colter finished her work in New Mexico, she returned to Grand Canyon to design the remarkable Hermit's Rest.

As with all the new Harvey buildings, various designs were considered. One of them was for a Swiss chalet with gingerbread trim. New building proposals were frequently in the alpine style of El Tovar, and there was ambivalence at Fred Harvey about whether to continue that style or build more of the indigenous-looking stone buildings that Colter favored and had originated in Hopi House. When the final decision was made, the company chose Colter's primitive stone building style.

The entrance path to Hermit's Rest went through an arch of haphazardly piled stones. Under the arch hung a broken mission bell that Colter had brought from New Mexico. A lantern hung from one of the projecting stones to guide the weary traveler to this place of rest.

Hermit's Rest was designed to look like a dwelling constructed by an untrained mountain man using the natural timber and boulders of the area. From the entrance path the structure looked almost haphazard, a jumble of stones with a protruding chimney spire. The front of the building had a porch that extended to the very edge of the canyon. A low stone wall protected visitors from the precipitous drop. The log beams of the porch were supported by crude posts hand-hewn from trees, the bark and limbs removed. The porch furniture was made from twisted tree stumps with seats or tabletops added. Seen from the west, the building barely protruded from the hillside; it was designed to merge with the natural surroundings. Colter did not want it to distract from the awesome beauty of the canyon itself.

The focal point inside Hermit's Rest was the fireplace built under a vaulted ceiling within an enormous stone arch. The fireplace stones within the arch were covered with soot, which made the building seem centuries old. A row of large glass windows along the front opened the room to a view of the canyon, and clerestory windows above them prevented the room from being gloomy. Colter's touch was apparent not only in the imaginative concept of the whole structure, but in the simple, rustic details that completed the interior: the wrought-iron wall candelabra and hanging metal lanterns, the chairs that were made from hollowed-out logs, and the medieval-looking andirons. The fireplace itself had an unusual center stone — large, face-like, ghostly. In front of the fireplace lay a large bearskin rug in open-jawed splendor.

For thirteen thousand dollars, the Fred Harvey Company had a refreshment place for their sightseeing tours. Here, passengers on the tour were served free tea and wafers; other visitors had to pay fifty cents. When Hermit's Rest opened in 1914, some of the railroad men teased Mary Colter about the building's rustic appearance. It was so dingy and full of cobwebs, they complained. "Why don't you clean up this place?" Colter laughed, "You can't imagine what it cost to make it look this old."[4]

The same year that Hermit's Rest was completed, another Colter building was opened. The Lookout was built on a precipice west of El Tovar, near the Kolbs' studio. It was designed as a place from which people could view and photograph the canyon. On the porch were high-powered telescopes providing visitors with a closer view of the gorge. Inside, the Lookout was a neat, comfortable, rustic studio of stone and log timbers. It contained a fireplace alcove and an art room where postcards, photographs, and paintings were for sale. Colter had designed the exterior stonework to resemble an indigenous primitive structure, similar to the ruins of ancient Indian dwellings found in the region. The chimney of the Lookout was a pile of stones, uneven at the top,

Entrance arch to Hermit's Rest

Hermit's Rest from the entrance path, taken in 1977

Porch of Hermit's Rest with bear trap and rustic furniture

Fireplace alcove at Hermit's Rest

Front windows looking out on the canyon from Hermit's Rest

hardly recognizable as a chimney. Weeds grew between the stones on the roof. Seen from a distance, the building became part of the canyon wall.

While development by both tourism and mining interests continued at Grand Canyon, legislators were considering ways to preserve the area. As early as 1882, a bill had been introduced in Congress to make Grand Canyon a national park. In 1905 the canyon was placed under the protection of the U.S. Forest Service, and seven years later Arizona became a state. In 1916 the Forest Service compiled the *Grand Canyon Working Plan* to establish some guidelines for future development at the canyon. Companies that had financial interests at the canyon outlined in this document their plans for expansion.

Fred Harvey submitted proposals for building tourist accommodations at Bright Angel Camp and at Indian Gardens, 3,200 feet down in the canyon. The plans and drawings of the proposed buildings for Indian Gardens are the only signed drawings by Mary Jane Colter extant today, but, ironically, the buildings were never built. Among the plans are some for various-sized guest houses accommodating from two to twelve persons. There is also a drawing of a large two-story guest house on the river, an expressionistic drawing of a Pueblo-style building with smoke from the chimney dramatically sweeping back into the canyon. Colter also had drawn plans for cottages of a proposed Cottage Community at the head of Bright Angel Trail. These plans were of use later in the 1930s when the Bright Angel Lodge area was developed. Indian Gardens,

however, was not developed by Fred Harvey, perhaps because World War I was on the horizon and economic conditions were uncertain.

In April of 1917 the United States entered World War I; in December of that year, President Wilson nationalized the rail system under the Federal Possession and Control Act to expedite the transportation of war material. The U.S. Railroad Administration ran the railways until 1920. During this time, luxury passenger service ended; the plans for building resort hotels were shelved until after the war. During this period, Colter had been at work on plans for El Navajo hotel at Gallup, New Mexico. Even the working plans had been drawn from Colter's designs by the railroad's chief engineer, E. A. Harrison, but the plans were put away for another five years until the war ended and tourist travel by rail resumed.

In February of 1919, the bill to make Grand Canyon a national park was signed by President Wilson. The establishment of the park was timely, given that a year before, developers in New York had tried to raise money to build a dam in the canyon for power production and irrigation. That effort had failed, and another project being promoted at that time — the construction of a scenic railroad along the south rim — was nullified by the new park regulations. The new restrictions limited mining, power, and reclamation projects to those "consistent with the primary purpose of the park."[5]

The park was created "to conserve the scenery and the natural and historic objects and the wild

The Lookout in its original form with jagged chimney and weeds on the roof, ca. 1914

High-powered telescope at the Lookout

Fireplace alcove and Art Room (right) in the Lookout

Colter's drawing of the Guest House at Indian Gardens, 1914

life therein and to provide for the enjoyment of the same in such manner and by such means as will leave them unimpaired for the enjoyment of future generations."[6] It was still possible for the railway to construct new buildings, but all proposals would be subject to much greater scrutiny. Most of the structures built for Fred Harvey from that time on were to replace or enlarge existing facilities. The days of unlimited development were over. When the concessioner for the new park was selected, Fred Harvey was chosen. The company had been established in business at Grand Canyon for more than fifteen years, so it continued to run the hotel, restaurants, and curio shops there.

In 1920, with World War I over, people began to travel again. Passenger travel on the Santa Fe Railway hit its peak. Visitors to Grand Canyon increased from 44,000 in 1919, to 100,000 in 1923, to 200,000 in 1929.

With the increase in visitors, Fred Harvey and the Santa Fe received approval to build Phantom Ranch at the bottom of the canyon. The 420-foot Kaibab swinging suspension bridge across the Colorado River was completed in 1921 and made the inner canyon more accessible. Fred Harvey offered mule trips into the canyon and needed accommodations for guests there, so Mary Colter drew up plans for Phantom Ranch.

The ranch consisted of a group of cabins built from the natural stone of the area. All other materials had to be brought in by mule. The facilities consisted of several individual cabins, a large dining hall, and a recreational hall. The cabins were simply furnished with two beds, a desk, and chair, but each had a fireplace and an Indian rug on the floor. The ranch could accommodate as many as seventy-five people. In later years the ranch grew its own pears, apples, grapes, and tomatoes, and raised chickens. Eight miles down the Kaibab Trail, Phantom Ranch became a favorite destination for hikers despite the five-thousand-foot descent and the summer temperatures of up to 120 degrees. The mule trip made the journey somewhat easier; visitors stayed overnight at the ranch and returned to the rim the following day. In the 1930s the Civilian Conservation Corps added a swimming pool to the ranch facilities, which was a welcomed treat for the weary muleriders and hikers. It was Colter who named the ranch after nearby Phantom Creek.[7]

When the ranch opened, Mary Coulter, at the age of fifty-three, and her sister Harriet, fifty-nine, took the mule trip down for the opening celebration. For Harriet the outing may have been more like an ordeal. She had not inherited Mary's vigor or good health. Always sickly, Harriet suffered from Bright's Disease, a kidney ailment, in the last years of her life. She nevertheless yielded to Mary's plan for both of them to take the arduous trip down to Phantom Ranch. She had always been Mary's best friend and supporter, and although she was six years older, she was dominated by her more assertive younger sister. Mary wanted Harriet to see her new buildings, and she undoubtedly thought the trip would be good for Harriet. Mary hadn't any patience with

Phantom Ranch in the Grand Canyon, 1922

people who just sat around and became invalids. Harriet survived the journey. Her name appears with Mary's in the guest registry.

M. E. J. Colter

Mary Colter's signature in the registry of Phantom Ranch, November 9, 1922

When she wasn't occupied with plans for new hotels, Colter was frequently remodeling the old ones. The Alvarado, nearly twenty years old, was renovated and expanded the same year that Phantom Ranch opened. Colter enlarged and redecorated the lounge and lobby, discarding the stiff, ponderous, black oak furniture and brightening the dark wainscoted interiors. She gave the restaurant a Spanish decor and completely renovated the lunchroom, covering the countertops with black Belgian glass that resembled onyx. Many of the original guest rooms had no baths, so ninety-four private baths were added. The hotel was not only modernized, but its famous Old World charm was also enhanced with the addition of fountains and lily ponds in the courtyard. The remodeling project, which lasted eight months and cost $300,000, doubled the capacity, making it the largest Fred Harvey hotel.[8]

The Alvarado was a popular spot in Albuquerque, not only for its own charm, but because famous people made a point of stopping there. When the train pulled into the station, local people would gather to see if there were any movie stars on board. It was a popular pastime to watch celebrities disembark from the train and enter the Alvarado or buy Indian souvenirs near the station until the "all aboard" called them back again. Stars like Douglas Fairbanks had their pictures taken at the Alvarado, wearing feathered headdresses and flanked by Indian children.

The Santa Fe trains evoked dreams of California and movie stars. "Ever see Los Angeles, Pasadena, Long Beach, Santa Monica, Catalina, or San Diego? Or Hollywood's movie studios? Ever hear the concerts in the new Hollywood Bowl or the mission bells at sunset?" ran the advertisement in the Chicago newspaper. The Santa Fe Railway promoted the California dream—Spanish missions, orange groves, sunshine, and Hollywood—which drew people to the West Coast by the thousands. Los Angeles grew from a population of 100,000 in 1900, to 500,000 in 1920, to one million in 1930. Everyone wanted to go to California, and the Santa Fe Railway wanted to take them there.

Above: El Navajo hotel and station, Gallup, New Mexico, opened 1923
Below: Architect's sketch of El Navajo, 1916

CHAPTER THREE

Buildings and Interiors
1922-1929

CALIFORNIA was not the only attraction. The Harveys could see that the Southwest also held great potential as a resort area. It was only a matter of time before vacationers from other parts of the country would discover the desert climate, the Indian festivals, and the great natural wonders like the Carlsbad Caverns and the Painted Desert. The Harveys envisioned building a chain of Santa Fe station hotels across the Southwest and providing sight-seeing tours from them with their own Santa Fe Transportation Company. Ford Harvey wrote to Byron in Chicago:

> You will note reference in my letter to Mr. Storey [Santa Fe Railway president] about the important influence of places like Gallup. The last time I saw him I discussed the advisability of facilities at Winslow, pointing out that with the right layout at Santa Fe, Albuquerque, Gallup, Winslow, Williams and Grand Canyon, we would be well equipped to take care of the motor development expected from the Santa Fe Transportation Company. It looks as if this motor business might grow rapidly and into important proportions. With Santa Fe and Albuquerque as bases for that territory, Gallup for Canyon de Chelly, Mesa Verde, Zuni, Inscription Rock, and other points of interest there, Winslow for the Petrified Forest, Hopi Villages and Painted Desert, the Meteorite Canyon and the White Mountain country, with Grand Canyon to take care of that section, there would be opportunity for

wide publicity and subsequent popular patronage — I am convinced there is quite a future there![1]

Byron relayed the message to Storey, and Storey agreed with their assessment.

At last, Colter was given the go-ahead for the new hotel in Gallup, New Mexico — El Navajo. She had finished the plans for it in 1916; they had been lying dormant for five years. The new building would be a departure from the other hotels with Spanish names and Spanish architecture: this hotel was to be a tribute to Native Americans. It was an extraordinary blending of modern architecture and ancient art.

Architectural historian David Gebhard described the exterior of the building as a "most vigorous modern statement. Horizontal and vertical grouping of windows, cubistic handling of walls and projecting balconies, and the three tasseled pair of lights attached to the main block of the building were design motifs which had become the vocabulary of the early modern movements in Europe and American architecture." It was a clear departure from the Spanish-Pueblo or California Mission Revival of El Ortiz and the Alvarado, and it was a bold step into modern architecture for Fred Harvey and the Santa Fe Railway.

Colter had established good relationships over the years with Indian artists and was consequently in a position to achieve a remarkable "first" in El Navajo: she was allowed to use Indian sand paintings as a decorative motif throughout the hotel. Prior to this, few non-Indians had ever seen sand paintings, for they were part of Navajo religious ritual and were destroyed after their use in ceremonies. The paintings were sacred and not for public scrutiny; records of their designs existed only in the memories of the medicine men who performed the sacred rituals. There were hundreds of different sand paintings that could be executed for nearly every human ill, joy, or necessity. They were used to cure the sick, avert evil, and petition for an unusual blessing. The medicine man directed the work as his assistants spread a field of white sand on the floor of his lodge and then made the drawing with colored sands. The patient or person requiring prayer was then seated on the sand painting. The assistants rubbed the colored sands on the patient, obliterating the design, but bringing the sand's curative powers to the one who needed it.

Sam Day, Jr., an Indian trader from St. Michaels, Arizona, drew the original sand painting sketches for El Navajo, and Fred Greer of the Harvey Company reproduced them on the walls of the hotel. Great care was taken to make the paintings authentic in every detail, and yet, at the reception for the opening of the hotel, a medicine man pointed to the leg of one of the male figures in the painting, *The Man Who Killed Fear*, and said, "You have omitted the rainbow garters." The error was promptly corrected. It was Colter's intention that the sand paintings be absolutely authentic and preserve this fragile art form for posterity.

Sand painting in El Navajo lobby, 1923

The paintings highlighted the smooth, plastered walls of the interior of the hotel with its long, low arches, black-and-red batik drapes, red tile floor, and bright Navajo rugs. On both sides of the fireplace in the reception lounge were distinctive wrought-iron wall lamps that Colter had designed using traditional Indian designs of clouds and lightning. The colors used throughout the hotel were subtle earth tones suggested by the natural mineral and vegetable dyes that Indian women used in fabrics and basketry. The overall effect was warm, spacious, and restful.

El Navajo was opened with an impressive House Blessing ceremonial. According to the announcement, "The Blessing of the House, The Ritual for Making Perfect, will be led by two of the oldest medicine men from the reservation, Little Singer and Little Stern Man."[2] Fred Harvey's Herman Schweizer; Mike Kirk, president of the Inter-Tribal Ceremonial Association; and Sam Day, Jr., planned the opening. When everyone had arrived, there were nearly two thousand Native Americans, including at least thirty medicine men from various tribes and a great number of sightseers and old-timers. Among the visitors was Henry Chee Dodge, chairman of the Navajo Tribal Council. Another visitor had been a companion of Kit Carson's, ninety-year-old Dan DuBoise, who under his white hair bore the scar from a scalping knife. Medicine men blessed the hotel, scattering pinches of pollen, sand, and sacred meal throughout the rooms to guard against evil and insure the well-being of the occupants. Old men,

many with white hair and bent with age, were active in the processional and dance. The Wind Ceremony was conducted by Hosteen Bi-men-m; Hash-Kay Yashi directed the Shooting Chant. The Night Chant and Mountain Chant were led by Ha-tia-le Yashi and Hosteen-bi-cha-tsohigi Bigay. It was a solemn, earnest, impressive ceremony. People came from far and near, even driving on the half-finished highway from Albuquerque, for the opening of El Navajo at Gallup, New Mexico, on May 26, 1923.

Five months after the opening of El Navajo, Harriet Colter died as her father had, suddenly, from a cerebral hemorrhage. She was sixty. Mary went to Altadena to attend to the necessary arrangements. The funeral was held in St. Paul at the home of a cousin, Alice Colter, and Harriet was buried in the family plot at Oakland Cemetery.

In 1923, at the age of fifty-four, Mary Jane Colter was alone. Her nearest relatives were cousins in St. Paul and Pittsburgh. She had friends in Kansas City, where she had worked and lived for nearly ten years; neighbors in Altadena; and associates at work, but they weren't family. The closest thing to family that she had now was the family of a former student whom she had taught at Mechanic Arts High School, Arthur Larkin. She had helped him work his way through high school, designing small wooden boxes for jewelry and larger boxes for sewing materials, which he had made and sold.

Lobby of El Navajo with sand paintings and distinctive wrought-iron wall lamps

When Arthur went on to the University of Minnesota on an athletic scholarship, she continued to be a friend and advisor. She attended his football games faithfully and even made suggestions for improving his performance as quarterback. After he had graduated with a degree in engineering and had married, Arthur Larkin still kept in touch; as the Larkin family grew, Colter became "Aunt Mary" to the Larkin children. The Larkins had, in fact, named their first daughter for her — Mary Colter Larkin. "Aunt Mary" sent the new baby a night lettergram in original verse for Valentine's Day:

To My own Valentine: If you ever love me as I now you, our bonds will be stronger than LePage's glue. I could not be sure that mine would be your first Valentine, but am hoping it will be your first telegram. Give Valentine love to your family.

Mary Colter

It was with the Larkins that she spent holidays. They were her family now.

But Colter was rarely at home. Her office was at the Fred Harvey headquarters in the Kansas City Union Terminal, and she had an apartment at Rockhill Manor, but she spent most of her time "out on the line" staying at one of the Harvey hotels along the Santa Fe line while working on a building project in the area. Her address was often in care of the Alvarado or El Tovar. She had a secretary, Sadie Rubins, who traveled with her, attending to a myriad of details and sending the night letter to Fred Harvey headquarters at the completion of each day's work.

Colter did some remodeling of the Alvarado in Albuquerque in 1924, but the big new project for her was the decoration of the Fred Harvey shops and restaurants at the new Chicago Union Terminal. There were restaurants and lunchrooms to decorate, as well as a group of small shops that catered to the needs of the traveler, whether for a haircut or aspirin, candy or reading material.

There were several Fred Harvey dining places in the terminal. The lunchroom could seat two hundred and serve five thousand meals a day. Amid the Corinthian columns, Colter arranged both square and round, green marble-topped tables with black leather chairs. She chose rubber tile for the floor to keep the room quiet. The walls were a cheerful light tan. As in all Fred Harvey dining rooms, the temperature was maintained at a comfortable seventy degrees. The Little Restaurant was a cozy tea room with brightly colored birds painted on the walls to heighten the sunporch atmosphere.

The Main Restaurant was more dignified. Colter made it a quiet, tasteful room with walnut wainscoting, comfortable Windsor chairs, soft lighting, and the traditional elegance of sterling silver, sparkling crystal, white linen, and fresh cut flowers. The room had the Old World atmosphere of a luxurious men's club, and epicurean meals were served. The foyer to the Main Restaurant provided Colter with a setting for the Chinese furnishings of which she

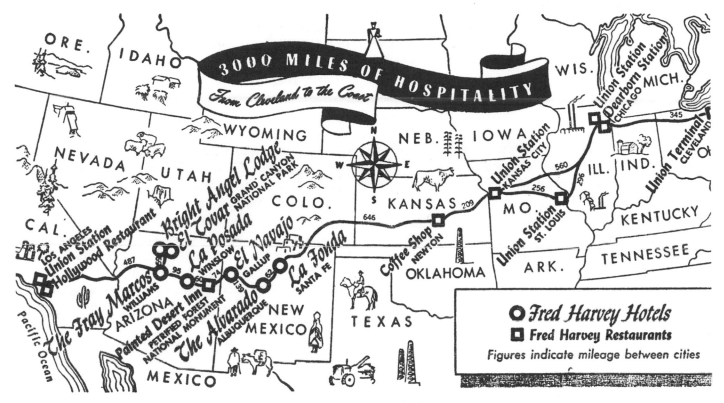

3,000 Miles of Hospitality

was particularly fond; she had furnished her own apartment with Chinese pieces. The foyer of the restaurant had a richly carved Chinese settee flanked by two Oriental ceramic elephants. A long gilt-framed mirror filled one wall, in front of which she placed an antique gold clock on a marble-topped table. The room was completed with a large vase of flowers near the door.

The cluster of Fred Harvey shops were called "minute shops" and were designed to provide quick service for the train traveler. Colter had some imaginative ideas for these shops, but there were problems, as always, in communicating with others about how to carry out the details. She wanted a large mirror to cover the door in one shop. The railroad engineers drawing the plans said it couldn't be done, that there would be no way to attach the doorknob. This obstacle was typical of the frustrations Colter encountered on the job. There were always a thousand details to be resolved in order to complete a project, and often the problems that arose were not so much problems of construction as problems of communication and cooperation.

In addition to being responsible for the interiors of the shops, she also designed the uniforms of the waitresses and salesclerks. The attire of the personnel was as important to the atmosphere of a room as was the decor, and she wanted the atmosphere to be right when the new facilities opened on July 23, 1925.

The Chicago station project was an important one. The Fred Harvey Company's Chicago offices were at the station, and Byron Harvey directed the dining car operations of the company from his office there. Colter naturally wanted these facilities at the station to please him, and sometimes pleasing the boss wasn't easy. Once, when Ford Harvey was away on a trip, Colter had redecorated the private dining room in Kansas City where he always ate. When he returned, he shouted in alarm, "Who put those curtains up? Get them out of here. They're spoiling my appetite."[3] The curtains were immediately replaced. Colter didn't want to repeat this experience with Byron in Chicago.

Some weeks before the Chicago Union Station opened, Mary Colter became sick and was confined to bed in her suite at the Blackstone Hotel. It was little more than a year after Harriet's death, and Mary had been working herself as hard as always, perhaps harder. The fatigue, sorrow, and frustration took their toll. Colter despised being ill. She had always been a little irritated with Harriet's ill health; she viewed being sick as a character flaw, a self-indulgence. As soon as she was able, she was out of bed and back at work.

The Santa Fe Railway had recently acquired the historic and colorful La Fonda hotel in Santa Fe, New Mexico. The Harvey Company would operate the hotel, and Colter's attention was again turned to the Southwest to plan the interior decoration of La Fonda.

While plans for the hotel were being made, Ford Harvey, president of the Fred Harvey Company, died. Ford's brother, Byron S. Harvey, became the

Bedroom suite at La Fonda with antique Spanish bed

new president, working out of his Chicago office. Ford's son, Frederick Henry Harvey, became a vice-president and continued the management of the company from the Kansas City headquarters. There were no other major personnel changes, and Colter kept her office in Kansas City.

While she was on her way to her office one morning, an accident nearly cost Mary Colter her life. The driver of the taxi taking her to work crashed head-on into an oncoming streetcar. Colter suffered facial cuts and injuries to her back and hip, but after x-rays and treatment at a hospital, she went home. With her new assignment in Santa Fe, the accident came at an inopportune time for Colter, putting her in a wheelchair for several weeks.

The newly acquired La Fonda hotel was at the end of the historic Santa Fe Trail, the pioneer route from the Missouri River to Santa Fe traveled by mules and wagon trains from 1821 on. The town of Santa Fe was older still, and the earliest description of it in 1610 mentions a *fonda*, or inn. The hotel that the railroad bought had had other names over the years — the U.S. Hotel and the Exchange Hotel. In 1919 the Exchange Hotel had been torn down to make way for La Fonda. The earlier building had had a colorful past. Its gambling casino had drawn a motley crowd of trappers, pioneers, soldiers, and politicians. For a time, a Confederate general and his staff had been quartered there, and at least one man, a chief justice, had been shot in the lobby, and another man was lynched in the backyard. General Kearney had held a victory ball there when the United States annexed New Mexico, and General U. S. Grant was entertained there at a ball after the Civil War. In April of 1919 the old adobe hotel was torn down. It was replaced by another building, which the railroad acquired in 1926 when the stock company owning it went broke.[4]

The hotel was built in the Spanish-Pueblo style developed by the conquering Spaniards, who adapted Indian pueblo architecture to their own needs by blending Moorish elements with Native American. The Pueblo Indians built with the natural materials at hand, pine logs and adobe mud. The sun-dried adobe eroded and lost its sharp edges in the wind and rain, producing the characteristic soft, rounded shape. Indian women had the job of adding more adobe to the walls to keep them in good repair, so the buildings were really hand-molded and shaped. In later buildings, the walls were hardened by the addition of lime. Builders eventually used cement stucco that resembled adobe but was durable and resisted erosion.

La Fonda was designed in 1920 by architects T. H. Rapp, W. M. Rapp, and A. C. Henrickson, who had designed the Santa Fe Art Museum three years before. La Fonda was constructed of earth-colored stucco to resemble adobe; it had a massive, rounded sculptural bulk, terraced roofs, open towers, wooden balconies, and rows of projecting vigas. Like the old Exchange Hotel, La Fonda was built around an open courtyard that contained a large, round fountain faced with Spanish tile. The Fred Harvey Company expanded the hotel from forty-six to one hundred

Interior patio with fountain at La Fonda, ca. 1929

fifty-six rooms by adding an annex and a fifth floor; this addition was designed by architect John Gaw Meem. An elevator was also installed, one of the first in Santa Fe.

Colter did away with the stiff, dowdy furniture that had darkened the lobby and redecorated it with an informal, warm, primarily Mexican decor. Every piece of furniture in the guest rooms, lounges, *portales* [porches], patio, lecture room, and cabaret was made according to her specifications. The furniture was shipped from Kansas City unfinished, and Colter brought Kansas City artist Earl Altaire to Santa Fe to hand paint it. He hand painted 798 pieces after Colter worked out the design and color scheme for each room on a separate sheet of paper. Each room had its own plan; no two rooms were the same. No two beds, except twin beds, had the same shape bedstead. In one room, the bullfight design hand painted on the front of the dresser was repeated in the rug in front of the dresser. In another, the design on a rug between the beds was repeated on the headboards. It was an enormous project to make each of the 156 rooms unique, but that was what Colter did.

She often found it difficult to get the effect she wanted, particularly when she wanted something unusual. The furniture makers balked when she wanted them to use the wrong side of the fabric. Then she had trouble with the company that was making some sheepskin cushions for her from blacksmith's aprons, because she wanted the cushions to have a used, sat-on appearance and the company wanted them to look new. She had the same problem with hooked rugs from North Carolina that had burros and bullfighters designed into them. She put them down on the floor for the workers and visitors to walk on in order to get rid of their new look. "We can't get the mellow effect until things have been used," she insisted.

Colter had Santa Fe artist Olive Rush decorate some of the rooms with murals and hand-painted glass. Vines and flowers were painted around some of the doorways and on the fireplaces in the bedrooms. Her New Mexican Room murals were a whimsical comment on life in New Mexico, featuring geraniums in an old lard pail, a goat stretching a long neck to munch a skirt on a clothesline, a gardener leaning lazily on a hoe while the corn stalks withered, a caballero serenading a señorita on a balcony, and matadors, cowboy boots, and prairie dogs scattered here and there. Colter had Rush and her students hand paint panels of glass, which she used in an interior door to give the colorful effect of a stained-glass window. The South Portal Lounge also had hand-painted glass between the large wooden beams in the ceiling. The light shone down in a bright rainbow of colors, making the lounge sunny and colorful even in winter.

Colter also made interesting use of traditional Mexican light fixtures made by a local tinsmith. All the light fixtures in the dining area were made of tin, the wall fixtures were electric candles backed by mirrors in tin frames, and the ceiling lights were

South Portal Lounge of La Fonda

tin stars. In the lounge, Colter added some humorous touches in metal — thin, wrought-iron jackrabbits holding ashtrays. She even included some iron plants. "I never thought the day would come when I would lean toward iron stags and cigar-store Indians, but those iron plants are so deserty looking I couldn't resist them." In a pot stood the green iron vegetation with blue iron blossoms large as a bucket. "And we may be glad to have them," she smiled, "after we have toiled to make . . . plants flourish in the patio."[5] Iron plants were better than none.

The most elegant and expensive furnishings were acquired for the suites on the fifth floor of the new annex. All the suites faced the outside rather than the courtyard, having a view of the Sangre de Cristo Mountains. Each had a fireplace and an open balcony and was furnished in costly antique Spanish furniture. The antique beds had originally been purchased from old homes in Spain by a decorator who planned to use them in a mansion being constructed in Florida. But before the beds arrived from Spain, a devastating storm struck Florida and swept away the unfinished mansion. When the beds did arrive, they were sold at auction.

The buyer knew I was much interested in these things and wrote me about them. After seeing them, I felt that they belonged at La Fonda and, while it is not customary to use such furniture in hotels, the temptation was too great. The bed in room 520 is a Catalan bed of the Eighteenth Century. Like all of the Catalan furniture of the Seventeenth and Eighteenth Centuries, it shows the French influence very plainly; this one being a good example of Directoire or Neo-Classic. As a matter of fact, the other genuine antique beds at La Fonda are of a much earlier period; the one in Suite 510 being a very unusual and beautiful example of Seventeenth Century.[6]

Suite 510 actually required two beds, so Colter had the master carpenter, E. V. Birt, make a replica of the antique, intricately carved headboard and all. The reproduction was so perfect that when the beds stood side by side, the antique and its copy were not discernible from each other.

A friend asked Mary Colter if she was at all apprehensive about decorating a major hotel in Santa Fe, a town full of artists. Colter confided, "I'm scared to death of these Santa Fe artists."[7] She needn't have worried. Fred Harvey opened the remodeled La Fonda in 1929, and it soon became a landmark. Not only did it become a mecca for tourists to the Southwest, but it was a haunt for Santa Feans as well. Mary Colter's achievement was all the more remarkable considering that she was still recovering from the Kansas City auto accident and had supervised the work at La Fonda almost entirely from a wheelchair.

La Fonda was also the headquarters of a service known as the Indian Detours. One wall of the courier's lounge just off the patio was covered with Gerald Cassidy's huge pictorial map of the Southwest showing the sights visited on these motor tours:

Indian Detour Harveycars at Cumbres Pass (photograph by Edward Kemp)

Indian Detour Harveycar stuck in the mud

Grand Canyon, Rainbow Bridge, Canyon de Chelly, The Painted Desert, Hopi mesas, Mesa Verde, Carlsbad Caverns, Ácoma, and others. There was also "a reflecting projection machine," which continuously showed scenes of New Mexico and the various trips offered on the Indian Detours. In the evening, free lectures about the culture and history of the Southwest were given in the beautiful Spanish-style lecture room.

A. Hunter Clarkson, whose father-in-law was a vice-president of the Santa Fe Railway, managed the Indian Detours. The Detours were originally conducted with a fleet of enormous Packards and Cadillacs, some with sixteen cylinders, called Harveycars. Each car had a driver and a courier who served as tour guide. The drivers dressed in riding breeches, boots, a ten-gallon hat, and a kerchief, while the couriers in the early days wore tailored gray uniforms. Later they wore skirts and velvet blouses and lots of Indian jewelry. The couriers were "refined and cultured young women of a corps admittedly unique in the travel world," according to the advertisement. The Detour began at the railway depot in Lamy, where the visitors were met and chauffeured to La Fonda in Santa Fe. The next day they were driven to one of the pueblos to see Indians making jewelry or pottery, and if it were a festival day, they could watch ceremonial dances. They were then returned to Lamy to continue their journey by rail. Originally, the tours were expensive and catered only to those of means, but as interest in them grew, all the major Harvey hotels in the Southwest initiated similar services. Visitors could leave the train and motor out to see Rainbow Bridge or the Painted Desert and then return to the comfort of a Fred Harvey hotel before continuing their journey.

The trips were always an adventure, sometimes inadvertently. The problem, in brief, was luxury cars on primitive roads. Getting huge Packards over dirt roads and around narrow mountain turns without incident was no small feat. Sometimes they got stuck in the sand, or a sudden rain would make it possible to get stuck in the mud instead. Engine trouble in the wilderness, hours from assistance, caused delays. After taking one of these trips, King Gillette, president of the safety razor company, wrote a letter to Fred Harvey in a fit of irritation. The Indian Detour car taking him to the Hopi Snake Dance had not arrived in time, and he had missed the dance. The Harvey Company received letters of complaint like that now and then. But they weren't, after all, running something as reliable as a train to Indian country. The Gillette letter was forwarded to Herman Schweizer, who had had his own misadventures traveling the roads through the Indian country to buy handicrafts for the curio shops. Schweizer wrote back lamely to the president of Fred Harvey, "Well, I always said these Snake Dance trips were difficult!"

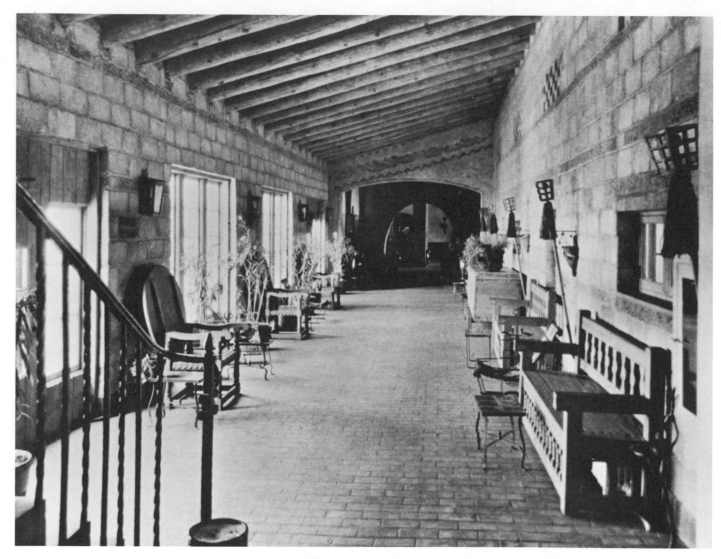

Cinder block court at La Posada

CHAPTER FOUR

Buildings and Interiors
1929 - 1941

THE SANTA FE RAILWAY had its greatest volume of passengers in 1920. After that, passenger traffic decreased every year except 1922. Competition from automobiles and buses reduced the number of passengers. Still convinced that the Southwest would become a prosperous tourist area, the Santa Fe and Fred Harvey continued to build resort hotels. The railway even increased its advertising about traveling in the Southwest in an attempt to lure passengers back to the trains.

Fred Harvey and the railway now had hotels in Santa Fe, Albuquerque, Gallup, Williams, and Grand Canyon. The last in that chain of resort hotels was to be at Winslow, in the eastern part of Arizona. Winslow was near the scenic areas of the Painted Desert and Petrified Forest, and only a half hour from Meteor Crater. Within driving distance of the Hopi pueblos where the Snake Dance was held annually, the hotel would provide a good starting point for Indian Detours. Moreover, all trains to Los Angeles went through Winslow. It seemed to be an advantageous location for a new hotel.

The station hotel at Winslow, La Posada, was an excellent example of Mary Colter's work. It was an expensive and beautiful building for which she did the architecture, the decorations, and even the landscaping. Of all her buildings, La Posada was closest to her heart.

Colter's philosophy was that a building should grow out of its setting, embodying the history and flavor of the location. It should belong to its environment as though indigenous to that spot. She could

La Posada and station, Winslow, Arizona, 1930

not visualize the design of a building or plan its decoration until she had thought out its "history." For La Posada she developed an elaborate history. It was to be like one of the large ranchos of the Southwest a century earlier, the residence of a wealthy Spanish *don* and his family. The building would be a large rambling ranch house set on eight acres of land, decorated and landscaped to suit the tastes of this affluent, educated, well-traveled family.

The furniture, consequently, was a mixture of crude pieces that might have been made by unskilled laborers on the ranch and elegant treasures that such a family would have brought home from their travels. There were hand-hewn benches and chairs next to a two-hundred-year-old antique chest that had once hauled grain from Spain to the New World. Rare old Spanish plates and Chinese copper jars stood inside a primitive Mexican *trastero* [cupboard]. Other treasures included blue-and-white Chinese Chippendale jars in the lobby and a fine old samovar in the dining room. One of the lampshades was made from a cardinal's umbrella. Many beautiful urns, pieces of china and earthenware, and copper and brass pots from Europe and Asia could be found throughout the building.

Since it was next to impossible to buy the furniture she wanted, Colter set up her own furniture factory in some rooms at the depot. There, master carpenter E. V. Birt and his crew of Mexican and Indian carpenters made "antique" furniture from Colter's designs. They carved the crude benches and Mexican-style wooden chandeliers as well as many fine, carefully finished pieces. For the lounge they made a copy of an old Spanish chair as well as beautiful walnut "Horseshoe" chairs with mulberry silk velour seatpads. They carved, upholstered, and antiqued new furniture to resemble the old, and they restored old pieces in need of repair. The beds and dressers designed by Colter were manufactured elsewhere and shipped to Winslow. There in the workshop the carpenters sandblasted them to age them and bring out their natural grain.

The hotel had seventy guest rooms and five suites. The wooden floors of these rooms were done in oak cut in random widths and pegged and grooved, characteristic of this early period. Each

Lobby of La Posada, 1930 (photograph by Gay M. Hamilton)

Interior of La Posada with iron-plant lights and the newsstand (center)

La Posada porch

room had a very old Spanish or Navajo rug. Some rooms had a corner fireplace with bright flowers and vines painted above the mantel. These decorations were done directly on the stucco in the Mexican manner by Earl Altaire. The draperies were home-spun in large floral patterns and bold colors. Each room had a picture of San Ysidro, patron saint of the inn. The linoleum block print had been done by Fred Greer after a very old carved-wood *santo* of San Ysidro, his oxen, and guardian angels. Colter designed the frames and E. V. Birt made them in the workshop. Since dressers had been virtually unheard of a century before, Colter created a substitute by adding drawers to old chests and putting painted tin Mexican mirrors on top.

The lounge had rare and unusual furnishings. Two high-backed divans upholstered in tapestry stood near the spacious fireplace; another divan had been a pew in an old Mexican church. Two tall wooden candlesticks copied from those in a Mexican church stood on either side of the hearth. A bearskin rug lay before the fireplace. On the wall were altar decorations from the church — palms of beaded flowers and colored tinsel, probably given to the church by a devoted family that had labored for months to make them. On the opposite wall were one-hundred-year-old Cortez engravings that depicted the discovery of America by the Spanish. The title and a brief history were written in gold leaf on the glass covering each engraving.

In the lobby and corridors of the hotel were very old benches and chairs, some dating back to the con-quistadors, others replicas. There also were copies of confessional stools and monk's chairs with painted chessboards on the back that turned down to form a table. The corridors of the guest rooms were made quiet by use of a rubberized linoleum that resembled tile. Windows with painted glass panes in the hall-ways allowed a mellow light to filter through. Darker corridors were lighted by iron flower floor lamps that resembled yucca plants, and throughout the hotel were Colter's amusing wrought-iron jack-rabbit standing ashtrays.

The pleasant dining room had a rough log-beamed ceiling and arched windows looking out onto the garden. Round tables on the dark tile floor were set with gold-colored linen, crystal, silver, and china with a black design. Looking down from a niche in the wall was the patron saint of the dining room, San Pasqual, the saint of feasts.

In addition to the dining room there was also a lunchroom that could seat one hundred and twenty people. Bright Spanish tile dominated the room. Colter had a company in Los Angeles copy old Spanish tile for use on the tables and countertops. The kitchen was the most modern electric kitchen to be found in 1930. Its bake shop, ice crusher, and dish-washer were all electric. La Posada featured the best Fred Harvey dining, delicious food served in gracious surroundings.

The exterior of the sprawling rancho had features that were typical of Spanish-style buildings done in the 1920s and '30s. Its tile roof, plastered walls, long portales, wrought-iron window grills,

Dining room of La Posada with San Pasquel (left), patron saint of feasts

La Posada lunchroom in Spanish tile (photograph by Gay M. Hamilton)

and balcony railings were all characteristic of the Spanish-Mediterranean buildings that had replaced the Mission style after 1915. Spanish Revival architecture spread throughout the United States but was particularly popular in those areas that had a Spanish past — Florida, California, and the Southwest.

La Posada was surrounded by acres of orchards and gardens. Just off the patio was a sunken garden with hidden shrines and with fountains, one of which flowed into a hollow stump of petrified wood. The rear of the building faced an expanse of lawn surrounding an ornate wrought-iron wishing well brought from Mexico in the 1890s. A large flower garden blossomed beyond the west wing of the building. Presiding over the garden was a life-size, hand-carved *bulto* [statue] of San Ysidro plowing with a yoke of oxen while guardian angels watched. Beyond the west garden, Colter built a high adobe wall like the ones used to protect the early ranchos; it even had the loopholes for guns. Near the wall she had planted a desert garden with native cacti and then added a dry well and an abandoned broken cart. Next to these was an old plains *carreta* with huge solid wooden wheels and yoke for oxen, like those that were dragged across the desert a century before. Rancho La Posada with its soft pink hue, the color of the earth at Winslow, was a place of history as well as beauty.

Finding a name for the hotel had been a problem. John F. Huckel usually found suitable names for Fred Harvey buildings. He wanted to call this latest hotel La Fonda, the inn, but that name had already been taken. He then chose El Ranchito, the little ranch, and the name was sent out in press releases to the newspapers. A telegram arrived almost immediately from the Winslow Chamber of Commerce expressing concern about the name of their new hotel. "For your information," the telegram read, "the name selected for the new hotel is widely used for houses of prostitution along the Mexican border."[1] Huckel found a new name in a hurry — La Posada, the resting place.

The planning and construction of La Posada had begun before the stock market crash of 1929, when the Santa Fe Railway and Fred Harvey were optimistic about economic growth. It seemed reasonable at the time to spend a considerable amount of money on the new station hotel, so they spent a million dollars to construct La Posada. But the Depression brought the railroad the worst losses in its history. La Posada opened in the midst of these hard times, and it is likely that the hotel never made money. When it opened on May 15, 1930, a railway official sent a telegram to the Fred Harvey Company, "Congratulations on the new building, La Posada. Hope income exceeds estimates as much as the building costs did."[2]

⌣•⌣

Now in her sixties, Mary Colter returned to Grand Canyon to create two new structures, an observation building and a hotel.

The Harvey Company needed a rest station-gift shop at the eastern end of its Grand Canyon sight-

Clay model of the Watchtower and kiva

seeing tours, twenty-five miles toward Cameron on the east rim drive. Colter wanted a structure that would be in harmony with this point overlooking Grand Canyon yet would provide the widest possible view of the area. She remembered the ruins of prehistoric towers found in various parts of the Southwest. Among the Mesa Verde cliff dwellings were the Round Tower of Cliff Palace and the Square Tower House. The Mummy Cave Cliff Dwelling at Canyon de Chelly also had towers. There were others at Hovenweep, Wupatki, Montezuma's Castle, and Betatakin. There was ample precedence for a tower.

In order to locate and study tower ruins, Colter chartered a small plane, an unusual and daring act at that time. After she had located the remains of a tower from the air, she would go overland by Harveycar to photograph and sketch it. For more than six months she studied the construction and masonry techniques of these prehistoric towers. Using her sketches and photographs, she then made a clay table-size model that was set in an exact replica of the terrain. Every bush and tree was in place, and the model assisted her in determining where alterations in the structure were desirable. On the site where the tower was to be constructed, she had a wooden platform built, seventy feet high, the same height as the proposed tower. With the wooden platform in place she could see if the height was agreeable to the setting and if it would provide the view she wanted.

There is more information about the Watchtower than any of Mary Colter's other buildings because she wrote a small handbook about it for the guides of the Harvey tours. The title indicates its scope — *Manual for Drivers and Guides Descriptive of the Indian Watchtower at Desert View and Its Relation, Architecturally, to the Prehistoric Ruins of the Southwest.* The one-hundred-page booklet gives a history of the ancient towers and kivas after which she patterned the Watchtower. The interior of the tower was decorated with Indian cave and wall drawings, and Colter gave a detailed account of what each represented and where it had been found. Consequently, the book is a treasure-trove of Indian symbols and legends. The book reveals some of Colter's personality as well: her scholarly approach to her work and her ability to make the subject clear and interesting. It is also apparent that she had a sense of humor.

The preface to the book was a letter from Colter to the men of the Grand Canyon Transportation Department who conducted the Fred Harvey sightseeing tours:

Dear Boys,

Different ones of you at different times have scolded me: "When are you going to tell us the meaning of the decorations in the Tower?" So it's your own fault if you are scared by the bulkiness of this manual — I'm only answering your own numerous insistent questions. But this is no reason for a general stampede! You aren't expected to learn it by heart.

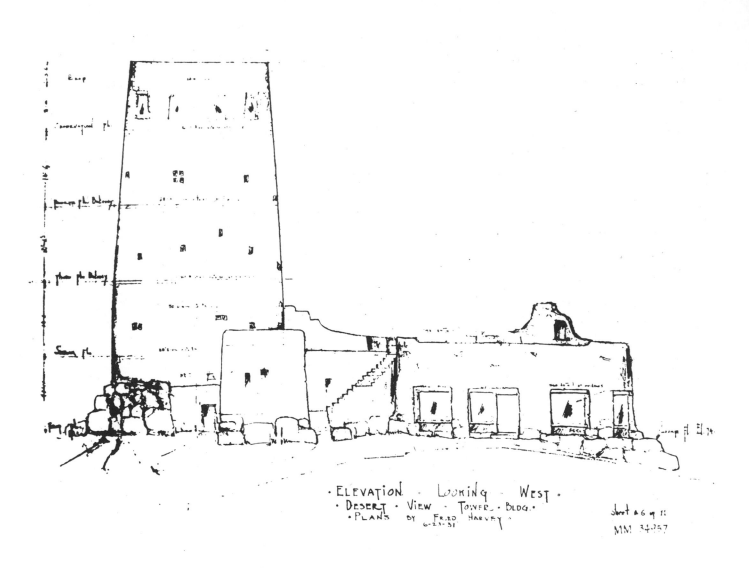

· ELEVATION · LOOKING · WEST ·
· DESERT · VIEW · TOWER · BLDG. ·
· PLANS · BY · FRED · HARVEY ·
6-23-31

Elevation looking west of Watchtower, drawn by Colter, 1931

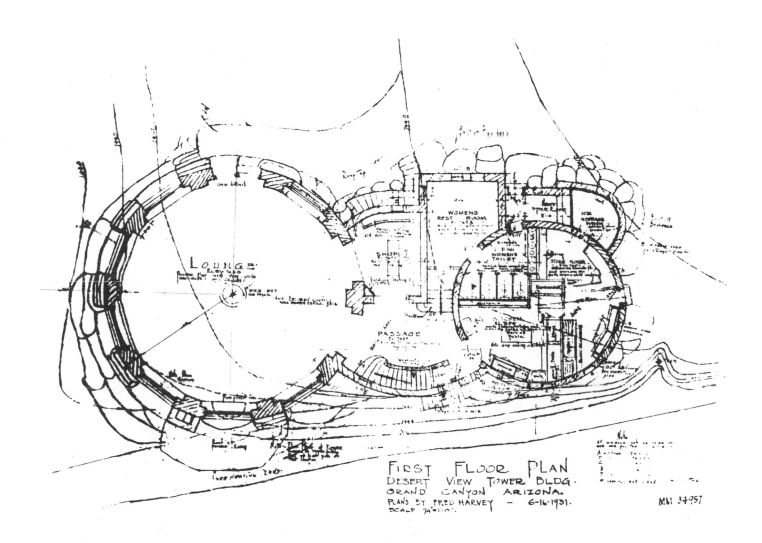

FIRST FLOOR PLAN
DESERT VIEW TOWER BLDG.
GRAND CANYON ARIZONA.
PLANS BY FRED HARVEY — 6-16-1931.
SCALE ¼"=1'-0".

First floor plan of Watchtower, drawn by Colter, 1931

Wooden platform erected prior to the construction
of the Watchtower, 1931

Construction of the Watchtower, 1932

She advised them to read it and familiarize themselves with the facts that they would want to use, and not to expect to be able to answer all the questions people would ask.

Considerable study will be necessary to tell about the decorations in the Tower, but you'll get lots of practice and it won't be long before you begin to rattle it off "parrot fashion" — and when it comes to that point, I won't love you any more!

She signed the letter, "Your very sincere friend and happy passenger, MEJC."

The Indian Watchtower at Desert View was not a copy, but what Colter called a "re-creation" of an Indian watchtower. At seventy feet it was taller than any known Indian tower and had a much greater diameter, being thirty feet at the base. It was unique in that it had a concrete foundation, and a steel framework made by the bridge department of the Santa Fe Railway. The steel framework was well hidden in the stones of the tower, but it gave the engineers a greater feeling of security about the structure than Indian-style mortared stones would have by themselves. Like the early towers, the Watchtower was made with natural stone found in the area so that it would blend into the environment. It was necessary to find rocks of just the right shape; stones that were chipped to shape had a different coloration on the interior than on their weathered exterior. Consequently, the stones had to be carefully, even painstakingly, selected. The smooth sur-

Balolookong stone on the Watchtower, taken 1977

face of the tower was broken with irregular rocks protruding every so often because they "create shadows and give more vigor to the walls."

Colter took into account the Indians' fondness for finding animal forms in oddly shaped stones by placing a large, grotesque-looking stone in the outer wall near the stairway. She called it *Balolookong*, after the mythical snake, the Great Plumed Serpent.

Inside the kiva of the Watchtower, 1932

Other strangely shaped stones were placed on a parapet of the kiva roof and in the interior of the building. She also included some genuine petroglyphs, ancient rocks bearing pecked designs, which were found near Ash Fork and Winslow, Arizona, placing them at the main entrance and outside the stairway wall.

The ground floor of the Watchtower was a large, round observation room with a spectacular view of the canyon. The room was modeled after an Indian kiva, with some additions for the comfort of the visitor, such as large viewing windows and a fireplace. Colter had also added some unusual furniture made from tree trunks and burls. Indian kivas are used for men's religious and social activities and are entered by ladder through an opening in the roof that also serves as a smoke hole for the fireplace. The Watchtower kiva had such a ladder to show how one traditionally entered a kiva, although it lacked the roof hole. The ladder went as far as the log ceiling, of which Colter was most proud; she had salvaged the logs from the old Grandview Hotel, the first hotel built at Grand Canyon.

From the kiva one could ascend stairs to the first floor of the tower, the Hopi Room. Legend has it that the Hopis came into the world through the Grand Canyon. They emerged through the *Sipapu*, a small opening somewhere in the deepest depth of the canyon, and the Hopis believe that their spirits will pass back through this opening after their deaths. Because of the close association of the Hopis with Grand Canyon, Colter wanted to feature their art and culture in the Watchtower. She had designs for the room in mind, but wanted a Hopi artist to do the artwork. A young Hopi named Fred Kabotie was a guide and musician at Grand Canyon; he was also a fine artist, and Colter was able to hire him to paint Hopi Room.

The Hopi Room took its theme from the traditional Hopi Snake Dance, a rain dance held in August. As Colter wrote, "Immediately the rain descends and the floods are opened — as many can affirm who have stalled in the arroyos on the way back to civilization after one of the weirdest experiences of a lifetime." A Snake Altar together with artifacts connected with the dance occupied the center of the room. The central feature of the altar was a sand painting. Crouched on the floor, Kabotie held colored sand between his thumb and two fingers and with infinite patience dribbled it into place. The workmanship was so fine that most people refused to believe that the picture was not painted with a brush. The work obviously required a steady hand and superb draftsmanship. Unlike traditional sand paintings used in ceremonies, this one was not brushed away upon completion. It was there under glass for people to see.

The central painting on the walls of Hopi Room was that of the Snake Legend. It recounted the beginning of the Snake Dances as well as the story of the first man to navigate the Colorado River. This voyage had occurred sometime in the legendary past. Elsewhere on the walls, Kabotie painted the God of Germination, the Star Priest, and the Little War God, representing other Hopi legends. On the ceiling he drew the symbols of stars and constellations taught to him by his grandmother when he was a small boy. The room was completed with a border design in a circle on the ceiling above the Snake Altar. It was the Great Snake, parent of all serpents.

Kabotie was thirty years old when he painted Hopi Room. In the years that followed he became an internationally known artist. In later years he wrote about his experience working with Mary Jane Colter at the Watchtower:

> Miss Colter was a very talented decorator with strong opinions, and quite elderly. I admired her work, and we got along well . . . most of the time. But once in awhile she would be difficult, especially when it came to matching colors. I remember one day she kept sending me up in the tower with little dabs of oil colors, too small to match. I don't know whether you'd call her thrifty or stingy, but I finally lost my patience. "Let me have that tube," I said, and slashed it open. I squeezed everything out, and stirred in the color I felt was right. "We're through — you've ruined everything," she gasped. "And you've used up all the paint!" "But Miss Colter, we haven't tried it yet," I said. I took a little dab and ran back up in the tower. Fortunately it matched, the very color we'd been seeking. So that saved my life — and hers.[3]

Colter was a perfectionist. She could be dogmatic and intractable. She knew the effect she wanted to achieve in a project and pursued it relentlessly. And nothing escaped her scrutiny. "She was a most energetic person and on many days was at the job site from early morning until late afternoon."[4] She supervised the placement of virtually every stone in the Watchtower and had the workmen tear out a section and do it again if it didn't look right. At that time, she was a sixty-year-old woman who had spent a lifetime advocating and defending her aesthetic vision, and she was not about to be deterred by opposition, whether it came from company officials, contractors, or stonemasons.

She was not an easy person to get along with. "Everyone hated to see her come on the job," one employee recalled; just her presence was a disturbing element. "I did not enjoy working with her. My admiration and affection came after both of us had retired," another co-worker, Harold Belt reflected. "Like most creative people and people of large accomplishment, she was very demanding of those over whom she had authority."[5] She had developed an imperious manner over the years; it may have been her way of coping with the problem of being a woman whose job required her to supervise men. Being the only woman executive, she was in an unusual situation in the company and had developed her

Fred Kabotie painting the Snake Legend in the Hopi Room of the Watchtower

own way of dealing with it. Undoubtedly, she contributed in some degree to her own lack of popularity by calling the men who worked for her — draftsmen and engineers — her "boys." She may have thought that her advanced years permitted her to use this term, but the men resented it. In return she was referred to as "Old Lady Colter," although never to her face.

Company officials varied in their regard for her. Some of the railroad officials she worked with found her "cantankerous" and "difficult to control on designs and budget." Others liked her. Her relationship with the Harveys was good. They recognized her talent and virtually gave her a free hand. But Colter had a running battle with her boss, John F. Huckel. "They fought for thirty years, and still they were friends and admirers," Huckel's secretary recalled. Like John Huckel and Fred Kabotie, many who clashed with Mary Colter still respected her and appreciated her talent.

⌣•⌣

The galleries above Hopi Room were reached by a stairway that curved upward along the inner wall of the tower. Fred Greer painted these two galleries with drawings from ancient kivas, caves, and cliff walls. Colter had canvassed every source in the Southwest to find these ancient drawings. The animal and human figures used to decorate the ceiling of the tower were adapted from very ancient rock paintings found at the Abo caves in central New Mexico. Copies that Herman Schweizer had made of these cave drawings twenty-five years before were used for models. Colter had benches built into the walls of the galleries, giving visitors a place to sit and absorb the beauty of the tower interior. Here they could observe the graceful curve of the circular stairway, the soft mauve and rust colors of the walls, and the light reflecting upward brightening the galleries above, and they could listen to the echo of sounds within.

The roof of the tower provided a panoramic view — the Grand Canyon with the Colorado River winding through Marble Gorge, the Painted Desert to the east, the Kaibab National Forest, and the San Francisco Peaks forty miles to the south. The tower top was the highest point on the south rim, 7,522 feet above sea level.

In boxes on the rooftop and attached to the viewing windows inside the kiva were reflectoscopes. Colter added these clever devices to give visitors a better view of the canyon. Claude Lorrain, a seventeenth century French landscape painter, had invented the device, which consisted of a sheet of black glass hinged to a window frame like a shutter. The glass could be moved back and forth to reflect different views; the black mirror reduced the intensity of the daylight and decreased eyestrain. In the dark glass, the colors of the canyon appeared more vivid, and since the glass reflected only a small portion of the vast panorama, one could enjoy the beauty of the canyon a segment at a time.

The Watchtower, 1932

To the west of the Watchtower, Colter constructed a "ruin." She wanted people to see the condition in which most prehistoric towers were to be found, not upright like the Watchtower, but in a rubble of stone. The ruin simulated the sort of remains from which archaeologists work to piece together knowledge about past civilizations, the kind of ruins Colter had studied before constructing the tower. These ruins lent the appearance of antiquity to the Watchtower as though it were the remaining standing structure of an ancient community.

In her manual, Colter wrote about the builders of those ancient towers. "The primitive architect never intentionally copied anything but made every building suit its own conditions and each one differed from every other according to the character of the *site*, the *materials* that could be procured and the *purpose* for which the building was intended." Certainly Colter's own building practices were in agreement with these. She would have added one more precept — that the building embody the history and culture of the place as well.

The Watchtower was completed three years after the plans were drawn. The May 13, 1933, dedication ceremony was predictably impressive.

With a marvelous horizontal motion of their bodies the dancers whirl away from the Canyon's rim. The strange staccato chant of the Keeper of the Kiva, thanking the spirits for their presence, pierces the rhythmic rattle of the gourds in the dancers' hands and the soft clatter of the tortoise shells on their ankles pierces the hollow thudding of the tom-toms. Occasionally the chant is interrupted by a cry from the leader of the dancers — a coyote cry, falsetto and unearthly.[6]

After the Watchtower and kiva were blessed, the dancers distributed rolls of blue piki bread to bless the audience. Then there were more dances — war dances, corn dances, dances until the "ruddy glare of colors in the Grand Canyon below fade into mauve and silver with blue-black shadows."[7] The colorful event made excellent publicity for Fred Harvey. It was covered by 620 newspapers from forty-five states, broadcast on the radio, and filmed for Paramount news.

Before starting work on her next project, Colter decorated the cocktail lounge at El Tovar with some humorous decorative touches, which are still there: a collection of ceramic roosters and some witty cowboy etchings.

With the Watchtower completed, Colter began work on the construction of Bright Angel Lodge. The new lodge was to be built on the historic site of the old Bright Angel Camp with its antiquated Bright Angel Hotel and cluster of cabins and tents. When the Santa Fe Railway completed its line to Grand Canyon, it had acquired the old Bright Angel Hotel, which had been built in the 1890s by John Hance, a picturesque old-timer at the canyon. Many

Old Bright Angel Camp with Bright Angel Hotel (right) and cabins, 1922

early settlers at Grand Canyon were unhappy with the arrival of the railroad; the leading hotel, the Grandview, was put out of business when the railroad built its terminal eleven miles away and opened its own hotel close to the station. The stagecoaches that used to take passengers from Flagstaff to the Grandview Hotel found that they couldn't compete with the trains and so ended their service. Thus, the Grandview was without customers and finally was forced to close.

Ralph Cameron, who had been a partner in a copper mine with Peter Berry, owner of the Grandview Hotel, had had his own running battle with the railroad for years. Cameron, his brother, and Berry had built the Bright Angel Trail in 1891 over an old Havasupai trail, primarily to get to the copper mines in the canyon. Cameron knew the value of such a trail and charged a toll of one dollar to the miners and tourists who used it. The Santa Fe objected to Cameron's toll, particularly since they intended to build a hotel close to the trail. Thus, the struggle began. Cameron built a hotel close to the Santa Fe station in order to cash in on the tourist trade brought by the railroad; the railroad moved its terminal further east so that passengers would have to pass their hotel before getting to Cameron's. Cameron retaliated by establishing mining claims on the land on which the Santa Fe intended to build the new hotel. He also filed mining claims at Indian Gardens, where the only spring and water source for the trail was located; and he put claims on some

of the most scenic points on the rim of the canyon as well. These mining claims had no mineral value and Cameron eventually lost them, but he was able to tie up the railway in court suits for years.

The Santa Fe was not dissuaded by the unfriendly attitude of some of the canyon's residents. Grand Canyon was a profitable venture for both the railroad and Fred Harvey, and they had plans for expansion. Mary Colter had drawn up plans for the Bright Angel facilities as early as 1916 when the Forest Service compiled its *Grand Canyon Working Plan of 1916–17*. Other concerns had intervened, however, and the plans had not been used. Now Fred Harvey and the railroad were ready to proceed.

There were a variety of designs under consideration, and Colter did several clay models of stone buildings: one a crude, stone, two-tiered building with triangular windows, and the other a long, low building with short, rounded towers barely visible through the trees and vegetation. Both of these were striking in design and would have been impressive buildings, but neither was approved. Part of the problem may have been that Colter had designed them for the canyon rim, and the Park Service was becoming more restrictive about construction on the rim. They wanted visitors to be able to walk along the edge of the canyon without obstruction. Since Bright Angel Lodge was to be more moderately priced than El Tovar, Colter designed a pioneer-style building in natural wood tones like the older hotel. These designs met with approval. The plans

Clay model of proposed Bright Angel Lodge at the edge of Canyon

were drawn by E. A. Harrison in the Chicago office of the Santa Fe, the contracts were let, and the construction started.

The $500,000 Bright Angel Lodge facilities consisted not only of a new lodge with shops and restaurants, but also of a little village of individual cabins that included old buildings of historic importance. Colter was instrumental in saving them from destruction, arranging for the new buildings to be built around or added to those of historic significance. Among them was the first post office at Grand Canyon, a two-story log building that was scheduled to be torn down when the new post office was built. Colter wanted to save it because of its early "hand squared" log construction. The railroad purchased it from the government, and Colter made it one of the Bright Angel Lodge cabins. Another historic building she saved was a cabin where Buckey O'Neill had lived. He was a colorful, early-day sheriff who was one of Teddy Roosevelt's Rough Riders killed in Cuba. His cabin became part of a seventeen-room guest lodge that was given his name. The new additions were constructed of logs or adobe to look old, but they contained all the modern conveniences. Before construction began, Colter made a model of the project on a table six feet long. Every tree and bush was indicated as well as every building, built to scale and painted to indicate which building materials would be used — adobe, log, or stone. The model was useful in determining where to place structures to preserve not only the historic buildings, but also the trees, flowers, and shrubs.

The lodge was a large stone and log building with a long, sweeping, pitched roof. The front porch had six enormous log columns that forked at the top to support the log roofbeams. The walls were of native stone. Two old coach lamps lit the entrance steps. The entrance door swung open onto a lobby of rough wooden walls, flagstone floors, and a log ceiling with kerosene lamps hanging from the beams. A stone fireplace was recessed into the rear wall and flanked by benches where guests could warm themselves by the fire. Above the fireplace Colter placed a huge wooden thunderbird, painted and feathered. It was the Indian symbol of the Powers of the Air, and it had been the Fred Harvey trademark for the Indian Detours for twenty-five years. The thunderbird was the "bright angel" from the sky that greeted visitors to the lodge.

Beyond the lobby was the lounge, which had two enormous windows looking out onto the canyon, framed like huge pictures. Between them was Colter's remarkable "geological" fireplace. It was made of stone from the strata that formed the canyon itself. The great water-worn stones of the Colorado River, which were at the base of the canyon, formed the hearth of the fireplace. Each succeeding layer of the canyon's strata was then laid all the way up to the ceiling. The surface stratum of the canyon, Kaibab limestone, finished off the top of the ten-foot-high fireplace. The effect was strikingly original and handsome. In order to achieve accuracy, the stone had to be carefully selected by someone who knew the canyon's geology, then packed on

Bright Angel Lodge from the air, 1935

Entrance to Bright Angel Lodge, 1936

Construction of Bright Angel Lodge, 1935

Fred Harvey
General Office, Union Station
Kansas City, Mo.

At Los Angeles, Calif.
April 1st, 1935

Mr. Eddie McKie
Chief Ranger Naturalist
Grand Canyon, Arizona

Dear Mr. McKie:

   You deserted me last winter without even a good-bye ! When I found you were gone I postponed the building of the fireplaces till your return. There was a young man who told me you had passed the job on to him. I would have been willing to have him gather the rock if he'd been able to come to terms with the contractor, but I was not prepared to accept a substitute when it came to the building of it!

   I tried to see you before I came up to Los Angeles on very important business, but did not succeed and expected to get back in plenty of time. But the mason is now at the Canyon with nothing to do and I'm having to pay him for lost time so as soon as I get back Thursday morning, I'll have to get on the Lounge fireplace.

   Won't you please, in the meantime, check the rock Ed Cummings has collected and see if there are any important omissions. If so, Ed can get it before Thursday morning. And won't you please be on hand Thursday morning. I know the design I want but I depend entirely on you for the geology.

   You know I am not trying to show every strata + variation in every part of the whole Canyon, - only those that occur either on the Bright Angel or the South Rim part of the Kaibab trails. I want it to be as authentic and therefore interesting as possible of course.

   Apparently we are losing out on the fossil rock for the Lobby fireplace. It is too bad for it would have been a knockout. All the more I am interested in getting the best results from the "rim to Rim" fireplace in the Lounge and I am counting on you for this.

   Will see you soon.

        Sincerely yours,

        Mary E. J. Colter

       M. E. J. Colter

Letter to Edwin McKee (correct spelling)

The geological fireplace in the lounge of Bright Angel Lodge, 1935

mules and hauled up from the canyon. Colter relied on park naturalist Edwin D. McKee's expert knowledge for the project. When he left unexpectedly, she postponed the construction of the fireplace and wrote him a letter. With McKee's help, Colter was able to finish the project.

Colter made every effort to find pioneer furniture for the lodge. She wanted old stools and chairs that had been brought overland in covered wagons. She searched secondhand stores for kerosene lamps with opaque glass shades and bathtubs with legs, furniture which she had copied and reproduced. She found two enormous rocking chairs for the lounge. Another treasure was the crudely made hobbyhorse that had once belonged to the first pioneer child born in Arizona. A great find was the seven-foot-tall Jenny Lind wooden cigar-store figure, which advertised a popular cigar. It was one of only five in the United States and was valued at five thousand dollars. The wooden figure was so dry that quarts of oil had to be poured on it to keep it from cracking.

Colter was so particular about the colors she used in decorating that she sometimes mixed her own. For the interior trim of Bright Angel Lodge she made a special shade of blue, and she was so insistent that the painters mix the shade exactly as she wanted it that they dubbed it "Mary Jane Blue." She had found the color she wanted for the exterior of Bright Angel Lodge while in Mexico looking for furnishings. Two friends were with her, B. A. Teal, architect with the Santa Fe in Los Angeles, and his wife. During the journey they passed a weathered, gray-colored telephone pole, and Colter shouted that this was just the color she wanted for the exterior of Bright Angel Lodge. Teal obligingly tore off a good-sized strip from the pole for Colter to take back as a color sample.

For the opening of Bright Angel Lodge, Colter wanted to have the lobby decorated with every kind of western hat that she could find. She advertised that "Hats of every size, shape and complexion are wanted. In days of yore a man was known by the hat he kept on his forelock!" She was able to acquire twenty-five hats of famous westerners, among them Pancho Villa's sombrero.

Two thousand people came to the barbecue that celebrated the opening of Bright Angel Lodge on June 22, 1935. The crowd included Hopis, Navajos, and Supais, some of whom had come long distances by horseback. The Hopis did ceremonial dances in the afternoon, and that evening cowboys sang and entertained at the banquet attended by Arizona Governor B. B. Moeur, the superintendent of the park, Fred Harvey and Santa Fe officials, and guests.

Bright Angel Lodge, with its rustic charm and moderate prices, was an immediate success. It had cost $500,000 and had taken two years to construct, but the additional rooms were promptly filled with guests. Visitors to the park were again as numerous as they had been in the years before the Depression; in another two years, 300,000 people would be visiting the park annually. Most were coming by car rather than train, and new roads were being constructed and old roads improved for easier access to the park. Even with the additional facilities at Bright Angel Lodge, accommodations were often insufficient for the number of visitors, particularly during the summer.

Prior to construction of the Lodge, the Santa Fe attempted to solve the continuing problem of insufficient water. The railway had been carrying water to the park every day by train since El Tovar had opened in 1905. With the expansion at Bright Angel, more water was needed, and the best source was the spring at Indian Gardens, 3,200 feet below the south rim. The Santa Fe surveyed the area and in 1931 hired a contractor to run a pipeline from Indian Gardens to the rim of the canyon. A suspension cable was constructed to transport into the canyon the men and materials needed. Two and a half miles of pipe were laid, and the pumping station began pumping enough water to entirely eliminate the need for transporting water by train. Before the cableway was taken down in 1932, Mary Colter took the journey down to Indian Gardens, dropping precariously over the rim of the canyon in a wooden box held with cables by a great hook from the suspension cable. This adventure was captured in a snapshot taken of her and the men of the pipeline construction company on October 8, 1932.

With the completion of Bright Angel Lodge, Mary Colter returned to Kansas City. In March of 1936 John F. Huckel of the Fred Harvey Company died. Described as a "dynamo" by those who knew him, he had been an imaginative and energetic force in the company. He had directed the construction of the Fred Harvey hotels throughout the Southwest and the Fred Harvey facilities in the union stations at Kansas City, Cleveland, and Chicago. He had also developed the Fred Harvey Collection of Indian art. As an administrator, one of his outstanding qualities was that he encouraged and helped develop the talents of those who worked for him, such as Herman Schweizer of the Indian Department, and Mary Colter. Often these relationships were stormy. The disputes between Huckel and Colter were legendary, but this adversary relationship seemed to bring out the best in both of them, and beneath the surface disagreements was an abiding mutual admiration and respect. Huckel's death was a blow to Colter, as it was to others at Fred Harvey who had known his friendship and support.

The company had scarcely realized the loss of Huckel when Vice-President Frederick H. Harvey and his wife, Elizabeth Drage Harvey, were killed in a plane crash in Pennsylvania in April of 1936. The accident was particularly tragic, for Frederick was just forty and would have been the third generation of Harveys to take the reins of the company.

Colter had been in Kansas City for twenty years, and Frederick Harvey's family had lived there even longer. But the other branch of the Harvey family had lived in Chicago for as many years, and now that the two major administrators in Kansas City were gone, Byron S. Harvey decided to move the company headquarters to his offices in Chicago. Although it would be two years before the move took place, the Kansas City days were nearly over.

Colter going down to Indian Gardens on the cableway with construction men, 1932

The cableway to Indian Gardens, 1932

The project Colter was working on during these months was the decoration of the Fred Harvey diners on the Santa Fe's new train, the Super Chief. It was a fast new diesel, an exclusively first-class passenger train with large picture windows, air conditioning, plush interiors, and meals by Fred Harvey. The train had five Pullman cars, a diner, and a lounge, and it could accommodate one hundred and four passengers and a crew of twelve. The cars, each named after an Indian pueblo, were decorated with Indian sand painting motifs and large photographic murals of the Southwest.

For the tableware of the Fred Harvey diners, Colter wanted something that was very distinctive — Indian art, yet something unique. In southern New Mexico, archaeologists had recently unearthed one-thousand-year-old pottery of the Mimbreño Indians; Colter decided to reproduce designs from this ancient pottery on the new china. She had her secretary, Sadie Rubins, contact the major museums to gather information about the Mimbreños, and after thorough study, Colter created thirty-seven different decorations for the various pieces of china. She used not only the formal patterns but also the simple designs of birds, animals, and fish. These were produced in a rose hue on light tan pottery. Guy Cowan, ceramic sculptor, worked with Colter on the style of the individual pieces, which were produced by the Syracuse China Company. Colter designed the silver service and flatware as well, making the table settings on this modern dining car a reminder of the antiquity of the land and its art.

Mimbreño designs on Super Chief china, taken in 1977

The Fred Harvey facilities in the Kansas City Union Station that had been built during World War I needed renovation. In addition to the restaurants, Fred Harvey had opened a drugstore and novelty shop. No one had thought the shops would succeed; passengers didn't have time to shop. But these stores became so successful that Fred Harvey decided to include them in other union stations. Since Colter had done the original decorating at the Kansas City terminal, she now supervised the renovation of the dining room and the addition of a new cocktail lounge.

Colter wanted the rooms to be beautiful and also to reflect the history of Kansas City. She engaged Hildreth Meiere of New York to paint murals of the early days in Westport, the original settlement from which Kansas City grew and an important outfitting station for the covered wagon journeys west. One mural depicted the arrival of the steamboat *Missouri* to Westport Landing. In another, a woman watched as a covered wagon left for the West. Colter let the murals determine the color scheme for the room, choosing from them gray, dark blue, and gold, and using plum for an occasional accent. The cocktail lounge, known as the Westport Room, was pear shaped. For it Colter commissioned murals of a lighter mood, whimsical drawings of early-day figures. She designed the furniture herself to get the right shade of bleached aspen and Swedish birch to complement the murals. These new facilities at the Kansas City Union Station opened in June of 1937.

At the same time that she was working on the Westport Room, the dormitory at Grand Canyon that she had drawn up in 1925 was finally being constructed. This was a fifty-two-room men's dormitory for the Fred Harvey employees at the canyon. The building was completed in December of 1936 and the women's dormitory was begun in 1937. This was later renamed Colter Hall.

A year later, Fred Harvey moved its headquarters from Kansas City to Chicago. In 1940 Colter gave up the Kansas City apartment where she had lived for twenty-five years and had her Chinese antiques packed and sent to her house in Altadena. Most of her work was in the Southwest, and when it was necessary for her to be in Chicago, she would stay at the Drake or Blackstone Hotel. In Chicago there were new people in the administration of Fred Harvey. Someone from outside the company was hired to replace John Huckel, so Colter had someone new to contend with. These changes in living and working conditions were disruptive for someone now seventy-one years old.

She was in California much of that year and the next, working on the decoration of the Fred Harvey shops in the new union station in Los Angeles. The eleven-million-dollar terminal was designed in California-Spanish style by Donald and John Parkinson. It was jointly owned by three railroads: the Union Pacific, the Southern Pacific, and the Atchison, Topeka, and Santa Fe. The facilities included a restaurant, cocktail lounge, soda fountain, luncheonette,

Grand Canyon Station with El Tovar on the right and Colter Hall on the left

news- and cigar-stand, drugstore, gift and book shop, as well as a barbershop — all of which Colter was responsible for decorating.

The lunchroom was a challenge. It was a difficult task to make this cavernous room designed to serve 200 people appear to be a cozy place, but she did make it attractive, retaining the Indian flavor that had long been associated with the Santa Fe Railway. She adapted the Indian blanket zigzag pattern in red, black, and buff tiles for the floor. She also introduced what at the time was considered the look of the future, Art Deco, into the design of the wall vents and hanging light fixtures. She saw that abstract aboriginal designs and modernistic lines were quite compatible.

The beautiful eighteenth-century Spanish Provincial restaurant was elegant and formal and was praised by everyone but the waitresses. Colter didn't want to clutter the room with a lot of little serving tables, which she felt would ruin its appearance. The waitresses complained that they had no place to set their heavy trays while they were serving. As it was, they had to hold the tray and serve at the same time, an almost impossible feat that caused many waitresses to quit.[8]

The Los Angeles Union Station opened on May 7, 1939, with a week-long celebration including pageants and parades. The railroads invited the public to watch a free forty-five minute pageant, *Romance of the Rails*, which portrayed the building of the rails west from 1869 to 1939. Later in the week the History of Travel Parade featured early conveyances, from a horse-drawn trolley once used in Los Angeles to the first locomotive in California. A half-million observers watched, including the governor of California, the mayor of Los Angeles, and railroad presidents and officials. The railroads' newspaper announcement introduced the new concept of "romantic progress":

A few paces beyond the colorful old plaza of El Pueblo de Nuestra Señora la Reina de Los Angeles stands the railroads' contribution to the romantic progress that has made the Los Angeles of today — the new Los Angeles Union Passenger Station, which officially opens this Sunday, May 7.[9]

The new station was so beautiful that the managing board of the station refused to let Fred Harvey sell popcorn on the premises. They didn't want messy popcorn on the floor to spoil the beauty of the new building.

That year she also decorated a cocktail lounge as a riverboat steamer at the St. Louis Union Station.

In December of the same year, the big "family" event for Mary Colter was the wedding of Barbara Larkin, Arthur Larkin's daughter. The Larkins had become a family of means, a decided contrast to Arthur's impoverished high school days. Mary Colter had also prospered and wanted to give Barbara Larkin a substantial wedding gift. She wrote to Barbara and asked that she pick out the silver tea service of her choice and let Mary know what it was.

Lunchroom at the Los Angeles Union Station, 1945

Through her work as a decorator, Colter had the connections to buy the tea service directly from the company at the wholesale price. Barbara Larkin went to the leading silver store in Minneapolis, where the manager showed her all the tea services. When she had decided on one, the manager completed the paperwork for the sale. Barbara in embarrassment explained that her aunt would not be purchasing the tea service from the store, but directly from the company. The manager was incensed that he was being deprived of a commission on the sale. He wrote directly to the company explaining that Mary Jane Colter of Kansas City would be purchasing a tea service directly from the company and that he should receive the commission on the sale. The company then wrote to Mary Colter, which made her furious. She called the Larkins and exploded: Barbara was young and naive and didn't deserve a present nor to be getting married.

Colter could be hard on people, not only on her employees, but also on her close friends and relatives. A cousin of hers admitted, "Frankly, she wasn't a favorite person of ours, as she felt her artistic temperament entitled her to be brutally frank whenever she felt like it, and although we were proud of her, we did not love her."[10] The Larkins remember her visits when they were children: "Aunt Mary" arriving "like a queen on her throne," in the back seat of her blue Buick, which she called "The Blue Goose," chauffeured by her secretary, Sadie Rubins. "She was a little dictatorial and crotchety in her later years. She was impatient with young

folk and disciplined us," Arthur Larkin, Jr., remembers. "She thought it was her right since my father was 'her boy.'" "She was a difficult house guest because she wouldn't get dressed until Father was coming home, sometimes five or six in the evening," Mary Larkin Smith recalls. "She was used to hotel service, and that was hard on my mother."

When Colter arrived in Minneapolis for the prenuptial festivities it was obvious that the storm was not over. All the time that she was there, she was gracious and charming to the other Larkins and the groom and his family, but she never spoke to Barbara. Colter had gone to an antique silver shop in Minneapolis and purchased a very fine antique Sheffield tea service that was much more expensive than the tea service Barbara had selected. But she gave the gift, not to the bride, but to the groom. Attached was a note that read, "Dear Jim, your new Aunt Mary believes in equal rights and can't see why the bride gets everything. If you want to, you can let her use these." In later years, Barbara Larkin Cullen was able to forgive the wedding-gift incident and observe, "She was certainly an unusual woman, but I can't help but feel that my life was enriched, certainly, because of her, and I'm glad I knew her."

In 1940, a new cocktail lounge designed and decorated by Mary Colter was added to the old Alvarado Hotel in Albuquerque. It was called La Cocina Cantina and was decorated to resemble an early Spanish-Mexican kitchen of the Southwest. The room featured a whitewashed, handmade brick fireplace recessed in an alcove like those in the early ranchos. The plan was to serve Mexican food at the big open fireplace in this cozy room during the winter months. Colter searched for original Mexican tiles to use as patterns for copies, and during the search, a barrel of old tile letters was found in a cellar corner. She decided to use the letters on the walls of the Cocina Cantina to spell out old Spanish proverbs about eating and drinking. Above the bar was *"A vuestra salud"* [to your health], and in another room, "Not with whom you were born, but with whom you pasture." Another proverb advised guests to leave the party while the fun was at its height. Over the bar, Colter placed a collection of rare old bottles, some of great value. One made in 1852 was a miniature of the opera star Jenny Lind in her role as Marguerite. Two others were original Booze Log Cabin Whiskey bottles from 1840. Colter lighted the interior of the Cantina with drop lights placed in Mexican parrot cages.

The Cantina opened onto a flagstone patio with flowering plants and vines, lighted at night with four unusual lamps Colter had found in Mexico. The lamps had survived the fire that destroyed the hotel and racetrack at Agua Caliente, but the heat had fused the colored glass so that the lamps now produced an extraordinary iridescence of color. Rays of many colors also filled the interior of the Cantina from designs painted on the window panes by Fred Greer; these colored panes brought a rainbow of turquoise, magenta, deep purple, orange, and green into the Cantina with the afternoon sun.

Colter not only decorated the Cantina but designed uniforms for the waitresses as well, copies of authentic old Spanish dresses. She had the waitresses walk up and down the stairs so that she could be sure that their ruffled petticoats were the right length to swish into view on the second step. While Colter was checking the dresses, the colorful scarf that her secretary was wearing caught her attention. She promptly confiscated the scarf and turned it into an apron for one of the barmaids; it was just the touch she was looking for.

CHAPTER FIVE

Working in Retirement
1941 - 1958

I N 1941 the United States entered World War II. The railway went on war duty, transporting troops and supplies across the country, and Fred Harvey was busy feeding the troops. Some of the Harvey Houses that had been closed due to a decline in tourism now opened to provide food for the military passengers. But vacationers for the resort hotel and Indian Detour business were nonexistent for the duration of the war. The expansion program of building new hotels across the Southwest was halted, and Colter had no new buildings to design or decorate for Fred Harvey.

During this period, Colter visited Mesa Verde National Park, a place known for its remarkable ruins of Indian cliff dwellings. She knew the park well, having spent time studying the construction methods and designs of early towers there when she was preparing to build the Watchtower at Grand Canyon. Colter loved this spot not only for its archaeological interest, but for the beauty of the setting amid the pines of southwest Colorado and for her friends in the Park Service who always treated her like visiting royalty. This trip she stayed in a small cabin, where she was quite comfortable until a thunderstorm struck. The roof needed repair, but it was war time and the Park Service had neither the supplies nor labor to fix leaky roofs. Colter summoned the manager; when he arrived, he found her sitting up in bed under an opened umbrella. To be sure that he understood her point clearly, she proceeded to lecture him on the absolutely unacceptable condition of her accommodations.

In November of 1943, another friend and associate at Fred Harvey died, Herman Schweizer, head of the Indian Department. He was seventy-three and had been with Fred Harvey since 1901, a year before Mary Colter began work for the company. She herself was now seventy-four. Many familiar faces were now gone, and she had seen many changes at Fred Harvey over the years. The company had once operated seventy-five Harvey Houses but now managed fewer than half that number. Dining cars and fast trains had closed many Harvey Houses; trains simply didn't need to stop as often. Then, too, train travel was not as popular as it had once been; rail passenger traffic continued to decline after World War II. The tourist spots of the Southwest that Fred Harvey and the railway had promoted were visited more frequently now by private automobile than by train, and the Santa Fe Railway survived by diversifying its business interests and moving into other economic activities. Since Fred Harvey had no plans for new Harvey Houses, in 1944 Mary Jane Colter decided to retire at the age of seventy-five.

She retired from the Santa Fe Railway on January 1, 1944, after twenty-nine and a half years of service as an architect and designer, but she kept her employment with Fred Harvey for a few more years. There might not be a need for new hotels, but there were always additions or alterations to be made in existing Harvey hotels and restaurants, and her talents as a decorator and designer would most certainly be needed.

The next few years were a time of transition: she was making plans for her eventual retirement from Fred Harvey, deciding where she wanted to live, sorting out and giving away things she didn't want to keep, and writing her will.

In 1946 with the war ended, tourism at Grand Canyon surged. Most people came by car; the passenger traffic of the railway continued to decline. But the resort hotel business at Grand Canyon prospered, and Colter was busy and at work again making alterations at Phantom Ranch.

The following year she had a new decorating project, the Painted Desert Inn. The inn was located in the Petrified Forest National Park near Holbrook, Arizona. It included a lunchroom, dining room, curio shop, and six small guest rooms with fireplaces. Built on the rim overlooking the Painted Desert at Kachina Point, the inn was constructed in Spanish-Pueblo style — plastered walls resembling Indian adobe with log vigas projecting from the walls, dark against the red earth-tones of the plaster. The building had been designed by Lyle Bennett and Lorimer H. Skidmore, architects for the National Park Service, and completed in 1938 by the Civilian Conservation Corps. Fred Harvey took over the concessions in 1947 and asked Colter to do the interiors. She used a Spanish-Indian motif: glass panes painted with Hopi pottery designs for the skylight, heavy hand-carved Mexican furniture in the dining room, and tin chandeliers for light fixtures. Colter asked Fred Kabotie, who had done the sand painting and murals at the Watchtower fifteen years before, to paint murals of Hopi Indian legends. In the dining areas of the Inn, he painted the Buffalo Dance and two other Hopi allegorical stories. Painted Desert Inn was a true Colter creation, combining the flavor of the Spanish Southwest with original Indian art. The surroundings were not only comfortable but were also a reminder of the region's cultural heritage.

With this job finished, Mary Colter prepared to retire completely. She was uncertain about where to live. She still owned the house in Altadena that she had purchased in 1916 and in which her sister Harriet had lived. It was on a quiet street on the slope of a hill overlooking Los Angeles, but Altadena, with all its sunny California weather, still didn't have the flavor of the Southwest. Years earlier she had purchased land in Sedona, Arizona, in the beautiful red rock country south of Flagstaff. She had thought of building a house there someday when she retired. It was in a remote and sparsely settled area. But the more she thought about it, the more Santa Fe seemed the best choice. The Southwest Regional Office of the National Park Service was in Santa Fe, and many of her friends who had worked for the Park Service at Grand Canyon had retired to Santa Fe. She had spent a lot of time there over the years while she was decorating La Fonda, and even earlier when she had decorated El Ortiz at Lamy. There were many people she knew and liked in Santa Fe; it was near the Indian pueblos and the Indian culture she loved. So Colter began looking for a home in Santa Fe and clearing out the house in Altadena.

In April 1947 she wrote to her friend Don Watson, park naturalist at Mesa Verde, that she had sold her Altadena house.

Altadena, California
April 12, 1947

Dear Don: —

Here I am still in California. I had expected to be back in Arizona and New Mexico a long time ago.

I have just sold "Ifcroft" — my Altadena house of many years and have commenced to pack up my many belongings. The question arises as to what to do with my Indian things like Baskets and Pots. My pottery is mainly Pueblo and I feel belongs in the Pueblo Country. As you know I favor the Mesa Verde Museum and that seems pretty close to home.

My pots have more than the usual significance in as much as I know the year in which every piece was *accquired and while some of it was . . . new — just out of the oven — on the day I got it; other pieces were very old and some of it prehistoric. The first piece *accquired in the collection was sent to me by friends who

*It takes 2 C's to spell the word in my estimation and I insist on 'em!

went to Ácoma in the year *1897*. Just fifty years ago! I have pieces of Hopi that I saw Maupais make and decorate in the years 1904 & 1905. I have owned all of it for over 40 years myself and have the date and place of buying of every piece. There are between two and three dozen pieces representing nearly every well known make. . . . (Haven't seen some of it for quite some time myself).

If you have a place for it I will send it to you. *Together* — it has considerable value — separated — it would just be pots — some of them very exceptional but some just ordinary. But I do not know how to get it to you. I can ship by truck to Gallup or Winslow but how to get it from there to Mesa Verde. Packed as carefully as necessary it will be pretty bulky. Do you people have a truck that could come after it to Winslow or Gallup or is there a public truck that would get it to you direct? And how should it be addressed? I have no one in either Winslow or Gallup to whom I could ship it as the Harvey Hotels have no storage space.

Now if you want it you will have to let me know right away. Return post. If you don't please let me know pronto anyway. Of course, I can sell it all or give it to the Southwest Museum out here but it does not seem to belong out here. It will go either to you or Jesse's Laboratory . . . or perhaps the Albuquerque University.

I have been having a regular siege with neuritis in my right arm and hand. Writing is very hard work — as is packing and work generally.

What did you think of my Jane? Well — she got a fine man in Frank Waters! I really believe his "Man Who Killed the Deer" comes closer to hitting the Bull's Eye than any other book on an Indian subject I have read.

I expect to get back to the Country around Albuquerque some time around the last of May. Where will you be? Hope to see you —

The very best ever to you —
Mary E. J. Colter

address for two weeks
526 E. Las Flores Dr.
Altadena — Calif.

Watson wrote back that he was interested in having the Indian pottery and baskets at Mesa Verde, and Colter sent them to him.

In 1948, at the age of seventy-nine, Mary Colter officially retired from Fred Harvey. She had been associated with the company for more than forty-six years since her first job in 1902, decorating the Indian Building in Albuquerque. She had seen the Southwest develop from a sparsely settled territory into a popular tourist area, and she had helped to popularize the region through the beautiful hotels and restaurants she had created for the rail-traveling public. These had been years of hard work and accomplishment. Now she was ready to retire.

But as it turned out, Fred Harvey still needed

La Cantinita in La Fonda, 1949

her. Just when she found a small house in Santa Fe at 2 Cerro Gordo and had barely moved in, Fred Harvey asked for her services one last time. La Fonda needed a new cocktail lounge, and no one was better qualified to design the lounge than Mary Colter, now a Santa Fe resident. She came out of retirement to do this last job for Fred Harvey.

For the cocktail lounge at La Fonda, Colter created another variation of the old Mexican kitchen and filled it with historic treasures. She had a fireplace built against one wall and had the wall buttresses covered with brick to make them look like ovens. The bricks she used were handmade, one hundred years old, from the old State Capitol. On the mantel she arranged some huge copper kettles gathered from the kitchen of the first Harvey House at Topeka; some of the kettles were eighty years old. The small cocktail tables for the room were made of solid walnut culled and cured for gun stocks during World War I. For the ceiling lights, Colter designed two unusual chandeliers resembling those used in Mexican inns years ago. They were metal racks in the shape of wagon wheels, with a candlestick at the end of each "spoke." In Mexican inns, such racks hung from the kitchen ceiling during the day. At bedtime they were lowered by pulley, and each guest took one of the candles to light the way to bed. Colter adapted this idea for La Cantinita, as the room was called. Colter always called the room her "pots and pans" room.

Colter's ideas often perplexed the construction men. An anecdote survives from the remodeling of La Cantinita: the contractor and the chief engineer for the railway, who were in charge of the project, went to lunch while the masons were building the brick wall. When the two men came back, they noticed how sloppy and irregular the wall was. They thought the masons must have been drinking. The contractor apologized to Colter; he would have it done over. "No, no," Colter replied, "that's just the way I want it."[1]

The creation of La Cantinita made it necessary to construct a new entrance to the hotel, and the walls of the long entranceway were ideal for a mural. Colter had Santa Fe artist Dorothy Stauffer depict the original La Fonda of the 1600s, including the Spanish caballeros, señoritas, Indians, and traders who inhabited Santa Fe in those times.

～‒ • ‒～

This job completed, Colter settled down to enjoy her retirement. She found a house that she liked better at 1 Plaza Chamisal, across the street from her friends the Miner Tillotsons. It was in a compound, a small Spanish-Indian adobe surrounded by lots of shrubs and trees. Now Colter had time to spend decorating her own home and arranging the extraordinary Indian and Chinese pieces she had gathered over the years. She unpacked her huge collection of books and spent time visiting with friends or reading — she had always been a great reader. And there was time for dinner parties with friends from the Park Service. Best of all, there were always friends who would go with her to the Indian

Last residence of Mary Colter in Santa Fe, New Mexico

dances. In thirty-four years she had never missed the Gallup ceremonials. In retirement she was financially secure: she received social security, a pension from Fred Harvey, another one from the Santa Fe, and had a pass to travel on the railroad any time she wished.[2]

There were, of course, the discomforts of old age — neuritis in her arm, insomnia, and false teeth that didn't fit properly. Colter never bothered to have her dentures adjusted, even though their clicking noise often irritated people listening to her talk. Those who knew her these later years invariably recall her loose dentures. A friend from Grand Canyon tells this story:

> Mary Jane Colter in later life had dental plates, and every time she would talk, they would just click and click. One day the manager of Fred Harvey Transportation was driving Mary Jane from Grand Canyon to the Del Rio Ranch operated by the Fred Harvey Company in Chino Valley. They were driving along and Mary Jane was talking and her teeth were clicking and clicking. Suddenly the manager, Earl Shirley, stopped the car, looked at Mary Jane and said, "Miss Colter, you are just going to have to remove your teeth or else you will have to walk the rest of the way." She removed her teeth and the car drove on.[3]

Getting to sleep was another problem. She found that a little whiskey in a glass of milk was better than sleeping pills, but she didn't like putting a lot of whiskey bottles in her garbage. She was concerned with what others might think. She would carry the bottles across the street to her neighbors, the Tillotsons, and leave the bottles in their garbage can.[4]

While unpacking and settling into her house in Santa Fe, Mary Colter sorted through the things she had gathered over the years. She wondered what to do with the Indian art she had collected; she hoped it could be put on display where the public might enjoy it. The pots and baskets she had collected had been sent to Mesa Verde National Park. Now she was looking over her extensive Indian jewelry collection and deciding what to do with it.

It was an extraordinary collection. She had been accumulating pieces since she first began to work for Fred Harvey, buying them at cost through the company. Herman Schweizer had made buying trips to the reservations frequently, sending the best pieces to Hopi House at Grand Canyon. Prominent people like William Randolph Hearst and George Horace Lorimer, editor of the *Saturday Evening Post*, were frequent visitors to the canyon, and they collected fine pieces of Indian art. Schweizer was at a loss to understand why the best pieces of jewelry were sold so fast, and when he checked with Frank Spencer, the manager, he learned that they were sold to Mary Jane Colter. She had Spencer bill the merchandise to her account in Kansas City, and all she paid was the actual cost of the item. From that day on, Colter was unable to buy the choice pieces at cost. Spencer kept them in the vault and showed them only to cash customers.[5] But Colter was undaunted. She was fascinated by Indian jewelry and went on collecting it the rest of her life. She always wore lots of it herself — rings on every finger and several necklaces at once. She loved to tell stories about how each piece was made and by whom. She had designed many pieces herself and had Indian craftsmen make them to her specifications.

In the spring of 1952, Colter's jewelry collection of more than a thousand pieces was displayed for the public at the Laboratory of Anthropology in Santa Fe. The Indian Arts Fund gave a party for her as a preview of the exhibition. It was a splendid occasion for Colter. She loved the conviviality of a party and dressing up with lots of rings and necklaces. On this occasion she wore her most spectacular pieces. One necklace was a double strand of the finest quality turquoise, a gift to her from the well-known Indian trader, Lorenzo Hubbell. She also wore a waist-long strand of multicolored wampum shells and turquoise beads. The coral inserts in the necklace were spines from the spiked oyster found in the Gulf of California and used by the Indians for trading. Besides the necklaces, she had a "path of truth" ring on her forefinger. It had three large, sky-blue turquoise stones flanked by stones the shape of footprints. Like handprints, these footprints were important symbols in both Navajo and Hopi art. On the other forefinger was a ring she had designed herself from an extra coral "hand" that had been leftover from a necklace she had commissioned. The Indian craftsman who made the ring had added a tiny turquoise band around the index finger of the coral "hand." Thus she had a ring on a ring.[6]

One of the displays at the exhibit was arranged to show the wide variety of animal and insect types that Indians used in their designs; seemingly all the creatures of the earth were represented. Among these pieces were prehistoric, carved bone turtles found in the Cottonwood area of Arizona. There were also beaded bone steer heads to be used as scarf holders, each one unique.

The necklaces on display had beads ranging in color from pure white to jet black. But not all of the black beads were jet: one necklace had "beads" made from the teeth of a black comb, not obsidian. In another, the beads were made from melted phonograph records that Indians had found in the ashes after a fiery train wreck. Colter said she knew that most museums would not collect pieces made of inferior material like phonograph records, but to her it was the artistic expression that was important, not the material.

After the Laboratory of Anthropology exhibition, Colter began cataloging her collection and having it appraised so that it could be given to the Mesa Verde Museum. She had had a siege of the flu again and was also having trouble with her eyes. She was feeling more of the infirmities of old age now and wanted to finish cataloging the jewelry collection. She didn't want the problem left for others to deal with after her death.

Don Watson, park naturalist at Mesa Verde, visited her in February of 1955 to help her catalog the jewelry. She had contacted C. G. Wallace of Zuni, New Mexico, to come to Santa Fe and appraise each piece of the collection, and she wanted Don to be there, too. Wallace came in March and went through more than 500 pieces of jewelry, many carved ox heads, shell bracelets, and bead necklaces, some from the thirteenth century. She wrote Don after he had returned to Mesa Verde that the collection was really not complete without an old silver bridle and belt. She asked him to find these items and she would pay for them.

Besides the jewelry, there were other possessions Mary Colter cared about that she wanted to give away so that others could make use of them. There was her extensive library. She had a fine collection of books on architecture, and a whole wall of over-size, expensive books — among them books about Spanish and Portuguese gardens, Chinese art, historic wallpapers, and the English home. She had complete collections of Shakespeare and O. Henry as well as books about Indian legends and history. Some were first editions. She donated most of the books, two hundred of them, to the Grand Canyon Community Library. The other possessions she was concerned about were some Sioux Indian drawings she had treasured since childhood. Made sometime before 1876, some were signatures; others represented an exploit or a joke and apparently had been drawn just for amusement's sake. Because she wanted to return the drawings to the land of the Sioux, Colter donated them to the Custer Battlefield National Monument.[7]

In the fall of 1954, Arthur Larkin died, an unexpected and severe blow for Mary Colter. He was fourteen years her junior and had always seemed to her to be a young man, having been her student. She had lost all of her own family years before, and now the head of her "adopted" family was gone. Scarcely had she dealt with this first grief when her neighbor and good friend, Miner Tillotson, died. She had known the Tillotson family since their Grand Canyon days, when Miner had been superintendent of the park and Colter was working on the Watchtower and Bright Angel Lodge. They had been friends for more than twenty years and neighbors for five. Tillotson's death came in February of 1955, only four months after Arthur Larkin's.

A week after Tillotson's death, Mary Colter fell and broke her hip while getting ready for bed. She may have had a small stroke. When the cook came in the morning to make breakfast, she found Mary where she had fallen the night before. It was a serious injury for someone now eighty-six years old. For many months she was bedridden, with three nurses tending her around the clock. Alvina Zimmerman took care of her correspondence and business matters. The hip eventually mended, but Colter never fully recovered her strength.

A year later, when she was able to deal with business matters again, Colter sent her jewelry collection to Mesa Verde. Since the Park Service had no money to buy display cases, she donated two thousand dollars to buy them. In her directions to the Park Service, she insisted that the jewelry not be displayed as a private "collection," but displayed to "emphasize the culture of the Indians of the Southwest, from prehistoric times to the most modern developments, as shown in their artifacts used for personal adornment."[8] The display cases were arranged in a way that the public could learn about and appreciate the artwork of Native Americans. They presented the history of Navajo and Pueblo jewelry, with necklaces from Santo Domingo, Laguna, Isleta, and other pueblos. The silver bridle and belt that Don Watson had bought at Colter's request were also displayed. One case contained various materials used in making jewelry — shell, turquoise, jet, and others — and showed how these materials were combined to make necklaces and pins. In another case, ancient and modern jewelry were used to show the evolution of the art over the years. It was a handsome, informative display that greatly enhanced the Mesa Verde Museum.

Mary Colter never saw the jewelry in its new home, but Carroll Burroughs, archaeologist at the park, visited her in Santa Fe and brought some snapshots of the display. It was a great satisfaction to Mary Colter to know that this Indian art that she had lovingly gathered over the years had now been returned to Indian country and placed where people might admire it and learn from it. Hers had been a long love affair with Indian art. She had enormous respect for it and joy in it. To be able to share its richness with others was her great delight.

During her convalescence, friends and associates from Fred Harvey would stop by to see her when they were in the area. They found her still in good spirits and bright of mind, although she was confined to a wheelchair.

On February 13, 1957, a newspaper advertisement in the Wall Street Journal read: "La Posada is for Sale! Santa Fe says losses make action necessary." The hotel and railroad station were put on the market at $400,000. The hotel included "eighty rooms, a coffee shop for 116, a dining room for seventy-two, a bar and a cocktail lounge. Just 166 miles from Grand Canyon."[9] Passenger traffic on the railroad had continued to decline since 1946, and the Santa Fe Railway had closed or sold many of its Harvey hotels and restaurants. For Mary Colter it was a tragedy: the most beautiful and best loved of all her buildings was to be dismantled and sold, the furniture to be auctioned off in Albuquerque. When La Posada closed, Colter observed, "There's such a thing as living too long."[10] In May of the same year El Navajo was torn down and the space used for a parking lot.

On January 8, 1958, at the age of eighty-eight, Mary Elizabeth Jane Colter died.

⌐•⌐

Colter's will, rewritten the year before her death, distributed her considerable estate to more than fifty persons and organizations. She had only a few relatives, some cousins in St. Paul and Pittsburgh. She left bequests for them as she did for her "adopted"

Mary Colter

family, the widow and children of Arthur Larkin. In her will she also remembered her doctor, lawyer, investment broker, secretary, cook, and many friends from Grand Canyon and Santa Fe, but also friends from her long-ago teaching days in St. Paul. A bequest to the daughter of the principal of Mechanic Arts High School was given, "In appreciation of the life-long friendship of her father, as well as affection for her." Some Fred Harvey tour drivers who had chauffeured her were given bequests, as was the son of one of the drivers, to pay for his education. To the janitor at her office in Kansas City she left $5,000. She had saved her money all her life and now she was generous not only to family and friends, but also to people who had served her and treated her kindly over the years. She left an estate of more than $150,000.

Mary Colter had accomplished much in her lifetime. She had created a score of impressive buildings throughout the Southwest, and she had advanced a new style of architecture that departed from the European ones that were in vogue, turning toward simpler, indigenous structures. Mary Colter's buildings had their roots in the American past, in the Indian and Spanish heritage of the Southwest that she loved.

Afterword

MANY OF Mary Jane Colter's buildings are gone now, torn down with the demise of passenger train travel. The Alvarado Hotel, Indian Building, and Museum became a parking lot. Only the remaining train station gives a hint of the spacious California mission-style building that once stood there. El Ortiz is gone. El Navajo is now a parking lot. The beautiful La Posada still stands, but the treasures Colter lavished on the interiors were sold at auction. The building itself was saved when the Santa Fe Railway decided to use it as a division headquarters. The beautiful lines of the exterior, the graceful arches, balconies, and spacious gardens — all these remain unchanged. Even in the interior, here and there, a Colter touch is recognizable: one can see flower murals on the stucco walls and colorful windows of hand-painted glass.

Traces of Colter's art linger on. The renowned La Fonda Hotel in Santa Fe is still open, although the interiors have been redecorated. And yet, a few Colter touches can still be seen: hand-painted glass panes in the door to the New Mexico Room, Arnold Ronnebeck's sculptured tiles of Indian ceremonial dances and Gerald Cassidy's Indian Detour map in the Santa Fe Room, and Dorothy Stauffer's mural in the entrance way to the hotel. La Cantinita, now a pastry shop, still has the Colter charm. The unusual candlestick chandeliers and the Mexican fireplace with a few old copper pots remain. Of all the places where she worked in the Southwest, Grand Canyon has the largest number of Colter buildings still standing. Six significant buildings remain: Hermit's Rest, the Lookout, Bright Angel Lodge, Phantom Ranch, Hopi House, and the Watchtower. In these structures one may still catch the spirit of the remarkable Mary Elizabeth Jane Colter.

Harriet and Mary Colter, ca. 1890

Notes

CHAPTER I

1. The California School of Design later became the Mark Hopkins Institute of Art and finally the San Francisco Art Institute. Mary Colter's school records were lost in the 1906 earthquake, which destroyed the Mark Hopkins mansion housing the Institute of Art.
2. Harold D. Mitchell, "Architecture in America: Its History Up to the Present Time," *California Architect and Building News*, February 1882, p. 29.
3. James Marshall, *Santa Fe: The Railroad That Built an Empire*, p. 109.
4. James D. Henderson, *"Meals by Fred Harvey,"* p. 28.
5. Charles Gleed, "The Rehabilitation of the Santa Fe Railway," *The Santa Fe Magazine*, December 1912, p. 24.
6. Byron Harvey III, "The Fred Harvey Collection: 1889–1963," *Plateau*, Fall 1963, p. 35.
7. Ibid.
8. The Fred Harvey Fine Arts Collection was given to the Heard Museum in Phoenix, Arizona.

CHAPTER II

1. Personal interview with Stewart Harvey, 28 June 1977.
2. Ibid.
3. Letter received from Alvin B. Teal, 21 December 1977.
4. Personal interview with Alvina Zimmerman, 27 June 1977.
5. J. Donald Hughes, *The Story of Man at Grand Canyon*, p. 129.
6. Ibid.
7. Personal interview with Preston Patraw, former Superintendent of Grand Canyon National Park, 28 June 1977. Another version of this story is that Harold Belt, John F. Huckel's secretary, named it.
8. "The Alvarado of Albuquerque, N.M.," *The Hotel Monthly*, October 1922, p. 50.

CHAPTER III

1. Ford Harvey letter to Byron Harvey, Kansas City, 21 February 1927. Fred Harvey files, Chicago.
2. *The Blessing of the House: Navajo House Blessing*, 25 May 1923, Fred Harvey Collection, Arizona State University.
3. Personal interview with Charles O. Coverly, 2 November 1977.
4. La Fonda Hotel brochure, *The Inn of History: An Account of La Fonda Since 1610*.
5. "La Fonda, Tripled in Size Becomes Spanish Fairyland," *The New Mexican*, 18 May 1929, p. 2.
6. "La Fonda, Santa Fe, New Mexico," *The Hotel Monthly*, March 1932, p. 24.
7. Personal interview with Hester Jones, 27 June 1977.

CHAPTER IV

1. Telephone interview with Harold A. Belt, 3 November 1977.
2. Ibid.
3. Fred Kabotie and Bill Belknap, *Fred Kabotie: Hopi Indian Artist*, p. 78–79.
4. Letter received from Frederick W. Witteborg, 7 February 1978.
5. Letter received from H. Belt, 10 December 1977.
6. Sallie Saunders, "Indian Watchtower at Grand Canyon is Dedicated by Hopi Indians," *The Santa Fe Magazine*, July 1933, p. 27.
7. Op. cit., p. 28.
8. Telephone interview with Herschel J. Stiffler, 7 November 1977.
9. "Los Angeles' New Union Station," *Los Angeles Times*, 1 May 1939, p. B.
10. Letter received from Alice Colter, 27 April 1977.

CHAPTER V

1. Letter received from Joseph A. Noble, 3 November 1977.
2. A. Zimmerman, loc. cit.
3. Letter received from Joseph Ernst, 12 February 1978.
4. A. Zimmerman, loc. cit.
5. J. Ernst, loc. cit.
6. "Miss Colter's Indian Jewels on Public Exhibition at Lab," *The New Mexican*, 18 April 1952, p. 6.
7. These drawings are now in the collection of Eastern Montana College.
8. M. Colter, Will, Coconino County Records, Arizona, p. 5.
9. "La Posada For Sale," *The Wall Street Journal*, 13 February 1957, p. 6.
10. Personal interview with Pauline and Preston Patraw, 28 June 1977.

Bibliography

PUBLISHED MATERIAL

"The Alvarado of Albuquerque, N.M." *The Hotel Monthly*, October 1922, p. 50.

Black, W. J. *Hotel El Tovar On the Rim of Grand Canyon.* Grand Canyon: Fred Harvey, 1909, revised 1977.

Cole, Doris. *From Tipi to Skyscraper.* Boston: i Press, inc., 1973.

Colter, Mary E. J. *Manual for Drivers and Guides Descriptive of the Indian Watchtower at Desert View and Its Relations, Architecturally, to the Prehistoric Ruins of the Southwest.* Grand Canyon: Fred Harvey, 1933.

"El Navajo Hotel Reflects the Painted Desert." *The Hotel Monthly*, July 1923, p. 40.

Fergusson, Erna. *Our Southwest.* New York: Alfred A. Knopf, 1940.

"Food Service on the Santa Fe's New Streamlined Trains." *The Hotel Monthly*, September 1938, p. 17–19.

Force, Kenneth. "Kansas City Likes Westport Room." *Restaurant Management*, February 1938, p. 82–85.

"Fred Harvey Caterer, Chicago Union Station." *The Hotel Monthly*, August 1925, p. 38.

"Fred Harvey Catering at Grand Canyon." *The Hotel Monthly*, October 1928, p. 31.

"Fred Harvey Welcomes You." *Los Angeles Times*, 3 May 1939, p. 6.

"Full Corps of Teachers, Mechanic Arts School Same as Last Year." *Globe*, 18 August 1898, p. 8.

Gebhard, David. "Architecture and the Fred Harvey Houses." *New Mexican Architect*, July–August 1962, p. 11–17.

Gebhard, David. "Architecture and the Fred Harvey Houses." *New Mexican Architect*, January–February 1964, p. 18–25.

Gleed, Charles S. "The Rehabilitation of the Santa Fe Railway." *The Santa Fe Magazine*, December 1912, p. 24.

Harvey, Byron, III. "The Fred Harvey Collection: 1889–1963." *Plateau*, Fall 1963, p. 35–53.

Henderson, James D. *Meals by Fred Harvey*. Fort Worth: Texas Christian University Press, 1969.

Hughes, J. Donald. *The Story of Man at Grand Canyon*. Grand Canyon: Grand Canyon Natural History Association, 1972.

"Impressions of El Ortiz." *The Santa Fe Magazine*, October 1910, p. 55.

"John F. Huckel, Fred Harvey Official, Passes Away." *The Santa Fe Magazine*, May 1936, p. 15.

Kabotie, Fred, and Belknap, Bill. *Fred Kabotie: Hopi Indian Artist*. Flagstaff: Northland Press, 1977.

La Fonda Hotel. *The Inn of History: An Account of La Fonda Since 1610*. Santa Fe: La Fonda Hotel, 1977.

"La Fonda, Santa Fe, New Mexico." *The Hotel Monthly*, March 1932, p. 24–29.

"La Fonda, Tripled in Size Becomes Spanish Fairyland." *The New Mexican*, 18 May 1929, p. 2.

"La Posada and Harveycars, Winslow." *The Hotel Monthly*, February 1931, p. 44.

"La Posada For Sale." *The Wall Street Journal*, 13 February 1957, p. 6.

"La Posada — 'The Resting Place.' " *Hospitality*. March 1949, p. 1.

"Los Angeles' New Union Station." *Los Angeles Times*, 1 May 1939, p. B.

Marshall, James. *Santa Fe: The Railroad That Built an Empire*. New York: Random House, 1945.

"Mary Colter Dies Here." *The New Mexican*, 8 January 1958, p. 2.

"Mary Jane Colter Helps Canyon Library." *The Arizona Republic*, 2 August 1957, p. 12.

Meadows, Amy. "Miss Colter Does It Again." *Hospitality*, September 1949, p. 3.

"Miss Colter Dies in Santa Fe." *Hospitality*, January–February 1958, p. 3.

"Miss Colter's Indian Jewels on Public Exhibition at Lab." *The New Mexican*, 18 April 1952, Sec. A, p. 6.

Mitchell, Harold D. "Architecture in America: Its History Up To The Present Time." *California Architect and Building News*, February 1882, p. 29.

National Park Service Rustic Architecture: 1916–1942. San Francisco: National Park Service, 1977.

"Navajo Sand Paintings as Decorative Motive." *El Palacio*, 15 June 1923, p. 175–83.

"The New Bright Angel Lodge and Cabins." *The Hotel Monthly*. December 1936, p. 13.

St. Paul City Directory 1884–85, St. Paul, Minnesota, p. 264.

Saunders, Sallie. "Indian Watchtower at Grand Canyon is Dedicated By Hopi Indians." *The Santa Fe Magazine*, July 1933, p. 27.

The Statistical History of the U.S. from Colonial Times to the Present. Stamford: Fairfield, 1960.

"Taxi Into Street Car." *The Kansas City Star*. 14 March 1929, p. 17.

"Union Station Still Magnet for Sight-Seeing Throngs." *Los Angeles Times*, 5 May 1939, Part II, p. 1.

U.S. Department of Interior, National Park Service, *Circular of General Information Regarding Grand Canyon National Park, Arizona*. Grand Canyon: National Park Service, 1929.

OTHER SOURCES

Atchison, Topeka, and Santa Fe Railway Collection, Bancroft Library, Berkeley, California.

California School of Design Minutes, 1873–1917, de-Young Museum, San Francisco, California.

Colter file, National Park Service Library, Grand Canyon, Arizona.

Colter file, National Park Service Library, Mesa Verde, Colorado.

Colter, Harriet. Death certificate, Los Angeles County Records, Los Angeles, California.

Colter, Mary E. J. Biographical sketch, Colter file, Heard Museum, Phoenix, Arizona.

Colter, Mary E. J. Will. Coconino County Records, Flagstaff, Arizona.

Colter, Rebecca. Death certificate, Seattle-King County Records, Seattle, Washington.

Colter, William. Death certificate, Nicollet County Records, St. Peter, Minnesota.

Fred Harvey Collection, The Hayden Papers, Arizona State University, Tempe, Arizona.

Fred Harvey Collection, Special Collections Library, University of Arizona, Tucson, Arizona.

Fred Harvey files, Fred Harvey, Chicago, Illinois.

Grand Canyon files, Western Regional Office Library, National Park Service, San Francisco, California.

Johnston, Don P. *Grand Canyon Working Plan, 1916*, National Park Service Library, Grand Canyon, Arizona.

Painted Desert files, Western Regional Office Library, National Park Service, San Francisco, California.

Records of the comptroller, Board of Education 1884–85, St. Paul Public Schools, St. Paul, Minnesota.

U.S. Census 1870, 17th Ward, Pittsburgh, Pennsylvania.

U.S. Census 1880, St. Paul, Minnesota.

INTERVIEWS

Belt, Harold A.	Telephone interview	3 November	1977
Bunting, Bainbridge	Personal interview	24 October	1977
Coverly, Charles O.	Personal interview	2 November	1977
Gilpin, Laura	Personal interview	25 October	1977
Guy, Ethel	Telephone interview	3 November	1977
Harvey Stewart	Personal interview	28 June	1977
Jones, Hester	Personal interview	27 June	1977
Larkin, Arthur E., Jr.	Personal interview	2 November	1977
Mead, Betty	Personal interview	28 June	1977
Patraw, Preston	Personal interview	28 June	1977
Patraw, Pauline	Personal interview	28 June	1977
Smith, Mary Colter Larkin	Telephone interview	16 February	1978
Stiffler, Herschel J.	Telephone interview	7 November	1977
Tiple, F. A.	Personal interview	1 November	1977
Turner, Helen	Personal interview	20 June	1977
Zimmerman, Alvina	Personal interview	27 June	1977

Telescope at the Lookout

PERSONAL LETTERS

Arnold, Edmund R.	Letters to author	31 October 1977; 17 March 1978
Belt, Harold A.	Letters to author	10 December 1977; 23 February 1978; 10 March 1978; 22 April 1978
Colter, Alice	Letters to author	27 April 1977; 9 January 1978
Colter, Mary E. J.	Telegram to Mary Colter Larkin	13 February 1913
	Letter to Edwin McKee	1 April 1935
	Letter to Don Watson	12 April 1947
	Letter to Mary Colter Larkin Smith	31 January 1952
	Letter to Mr. and Mrs. Preston Patraw	19 November 1954
Cullen, Barbara	Letters to author	13 November 1977; 17 April 1978
Ernst, Joseph	Letters to author	1 January 1978; 12 February 1978
Fowler, Zelma	Letters to author	1 March 1978; 8 April 1978
Harvey, Ford	Letter to Byron S. Harvey	21 February 1927
Manns, Timothy	Letter to author	14 February 1978
Naille, Carol	Letter to author	27 December 1977
Noble, Joseph A.	Letter to author	3 November 1977
Noonan, Martha	Letter to author	14 November 1977
Roche, George J.	Letter to author	2 January 1978
Schulze, Nina	Letters to author	2 January 1978; 25 April 1978
Teal, Alvin	Letters to author	21 December 1977; 16 January 1978; 10 March 1978
Tillotson, M. R.	Letter to M. E. J. Colter	20 January 1934
Van Noy, Joe Emma	Letters to author	30 March 1978; 21 April 1978
Witteborg, Frederick W.	Letter to author	7 February 1978
Zimmerman, Alvina	Letter to author	30 November 1977

The Alvarado torn down, March 1970 (photograph by Gordon Ferguson)

Mary Colter's Buildings

YEAR	PLACE	BUILDING	DESIGNER	STATUS
1902	Albuquerque	Alvarado	Charles F. Whittlesey, architect	down (1970)
		Indian Building	Colter, interior decorator	down (1970)
1905	Grand Canyon	Hopi House	Colter, architect and decorator	standing
1905	Grand Canyon	El Tovar	Charles F. Whittlesey, architect	standing
			Colter, decorator of cocktail lounge	
1910	Lamy, N.M.	El Ortiz	Louis Curtiss, architect	down (1943)
			Colter, interior decorator	
1913	Kansas City	Union Station	Colter, decorator of Fred Harvey shops	standing
1914	Grand Canyon	Lookout	Colter, architect and decorator	standing
1914	Grand Canyon	Hermit's Rest	Colter, architect and decorator	standing
1922	Grand Canyon	Phantom Ranch	Colter, architect and decorator	standing
1923	Gallup, N.M.	El Navajo	Colter, architect and decorator	down (1957)
1925	Chicago	Union Station	Colter, decorator of Fred Harvey shops	standing
1925	Santa Fe	La Fonda	T. H. Rapp, W. M. Rapp, and A. C. Henrickson, architects	standing
			Colter, interior decorator	

YEAR	PLACE	BUILDING	DESIGNER	STATUS
1930	Winslow, Ariz.	La Posada	Colter, architect and decorator	standing
1932	Grand Canyon	Watchtower	Colter, architect and decorator	standing
1935	Grand Canyon	Bright Angel Lodge	Colter, architect and decorator	standing
1936	Grand Canyon	Men's Dormitory	Colter, architect	standing
1937	Grand Canyon	Women's Dormitory	Colter, architect	standing
1937	Kansas City	Union Station	Colter, decorator of Westport Room	standing
1939	St. Louis	Union Station	Colter, decorator of Fred Harvey shops	standing
1939	Los Angeles	Union Station	Colter, decorator of Fred Harvey shops	standing
1940	Albuquerque	Alvarado	Colter, decorator of La Cosina Cantina	down (1970)
1947	Painted Desert	Painted Desert Inn	Colter, interior decorator	standing
1949	Santa Fe	La Fonda	Colter, decorator of La Cantinita	standing

Other buildings have been attributed to Mary Colter erroneously, such as
the Casa del Desierto at Barstow, California,
designed by architect Francis W. Wilson of Santa Barbara.

Index

Page numbers in italics indicate photographs.

COVER DESIGN BY LARRY LINDAHL
INTERIOR DESIGN BY NANCY SOLOMON
PRINTED AT NORTHLAND PRINTING
FLAGSTAFF, ARIZONA

GRAND CANYON NATURAL HISTORY ASSOCIATION
P.O. BOX 399, GRAND CANYON, ARIZONA 86023